The Beginning is Wisdom

Library of Congress Control Number: 2025905577

Published in the United States by: Brave Walrieux Publishing, Santa Cruz, California, USA

Edited by: Kristen Tatroe

Cover and Layout Design by: Derol Frye

ISBN: 9798992344516

2nd revised paperback edition.

The Beginning is Wisdom

Re-Symbolizing the Cornerstone of Freemasonry

PETER CARDILLA

BRAVE WALRIEUX PUBLISHING
Santa Cruz, California

For Kim, my wife and best friend.

Contents

ACKNOWLEDGEMENTS

A few people I'd like to thank.

For the great deal of encouragement, support, and inspiration you provided, my sincere thanks goes to the following people and groups:

My wife and collaborator in life, Dr. Kim Cardilla, for your daily support and enthusiasm, and your steady reassurance throughout this long process; my son, Quintin Cardilla, my first true and still my greatest inspiration, for never denying me an ear as I talked through my many ideas; my mother Marissa Mitchell Adorno who always made me feel like I could do anything I wanted; Michael and Pamela Mueller for your kindness and invaluable advice; Stephen and Alison Johannensen for reading the earliest manuscripts; John and Andrea Sigismondi—my beloved friends, mentors, and kindred spirits—for your unwavering support; Kristen Tatroe for your advice and support; Derol Frye for making me look good and for being my friend; Shawn Eyer for your feedback and generous help and advice; Danielle Christiano for a lifetime of love and encouragement; Michelle Adorno, who I always can't wait to see again; Christopher Willingham for teaching me so much and always leading me down the right path; Rabbi Shifra Weiss-Penzias for all you taught me and for showing me where to find the Kabbalah I was looking for; Matthew Kannely for your friendship, guidance, and countless hours of consultation; friend and author R.E. Sohl who graciously and generously indulged me in my earliest questions; Gary Butler and Two Birds Books in Pleasure Point; Bill, Chris, and Judy Dino from Red to Black Editing for your help and expertise; the Grand Lodge of Free and Accepted Masons of the State of California, especially Emily Limon and Jordan Yelinek, for the kind help and access to data; Robert Strohmeyer for encouraging these peculiar interests of mine; Jeff Wilkins for exemplifying the highest ideals of Freemasonry; Kenneth Nagel for your patronage, friendship, and trust; the members of Confidence Lodge #110 in Soquel, California and the members of Paideia Lodge #852 in Santa Cruz, California for your fellowship and brotherly love; San Jose Valley of the Ancient and Accepted Scottish Rite; Golden State College of the SRICF; and my friends, family, and brothers who supported me in this endeavor, Michael Baba, Rosemarie Cardilla, Michelle Cardilla, Fassio Elder, Gregg Hall, Jacob Imsland, Samuel Imsland, Gabriel Mariscal, Walter McCollum, Craig Peterson, Bud Ramsey, and Adam Reber.

For years, I wanted to write this book

I've wanted to write this book for years. To me, Masonry and Kabbalah go together like peanut butter and jelly. However, despite my enthusiasm, I wasn't entirely sure what to say. To start with, few people have heard of Kabbalah, and it's difficult to explain. Moreover, Freemasonry, even if it's the better known of the two, is still neither particularly well understood nor what you would call popular. Of course, there have always been freemasons interested in Kabbalah, but never very many.

Despite garnering relatively little interest, there's been a surprisingly large amount written on the subject. So, why should I write more? If I can't answer that question perfectly, I will say (maybe only trying to seem reasonable) that this book offers a new perspective.

A lot has been written connecting Kabbalah to Freemasonry. Much of it, however, is unreliable—especially concerning Kabbalah. With all due respect to the authors, these books, encyclopedia entries, magazine articles, and webpages are often misinformed. The modern study of Kabbalah has done great scholarly work. Much more is now known about the origins and development of Kabbalah, including a great deal that differs from past ideas. Little of this scholarship, however, has made it into the domain of masonic writing, where, unfortunately, outdated ideas are still too commonly reflected.

Kabbalah has, especially within Western traditions, long been miscategorized as alchemy and magic. Frequent mash-ups of occult symbols—some which include nothing authentic to Kabbalah—are still presented and accepted as genuine examples. However, this is not the Kabbalah I know. What I have found in Kabbalah is something I'd never experienced before: A way to contemplate the unimaginable and to believe the incredible, not with foolish credulity or blind faith, but in terms I could imagine, feel, and, most importantly, believe. It gave me a chance to have faith, an opportunity to believe. It gave me a God I *could* believe in.

Despite coming from cultures that are traditionally religious, my parents were not. As a child, I knew I was Catholic even if I didn't know exactly what that meant. My family didn't go to church unless a wedding or baptism obligated it, and we often joked in the harmless but irreverent ways common to nonreligious Catholics. My parents divorced when I was eight. My mother remarried, but nothing really changed. My stepfather was ethnically and culturally Jewish, but he, like us, was not religious. We celebrated holidays like a secular family, exchanging gifts, attending festivities, and ignoring most of the religious meaning.

By my teens, I didn't know what I believed, but it wasn't anything I'd been told at a church or temple. Nothing I had heard about God or religion was compelling, and I was convinced it was all nonsense. Every explanation I heard required me to deny something I believed or to admit something I didn't believe. I couldn't find a religion I could honestly embrace, and I strongly suspected there was no such thing.

As an adult, however, something changed. I realized I didn't have the answers to everything (only teenagers know that much). I had questions. The world felt bigger. The past seemed infinitely more mysterious. How did we get here? How did *anything* get here? I became intrigued with the past. Beyond history, I wondered about prehistory and the earliest humans who set themselves apart from the other animals. I was in awe of the achievements of people we often regard as primitive: the development of language, art, and society. I realized many displays of absolute genius responsible for the advancement of humanity are today taken for granted or simply unappreciated. Perhaps, I thought, there was something to be found in ancient wisdom after all.

I wondered about the future, too. Where are we going? Where *should* we be going? I recognized the value of hope and the benefits of ascribing meaning to one's life. I wanted a meaningful life. I wanted hope for the future. Not that I was living an unproductive or desperate life at the time; in fact, that was far from the case. I had a beautiful wife (I still do) and was living in a new state with a young child and a new career. I was plenty busy. Though I couldn't believe there was room for anything else, something was missing. I began searching for answers. I didn't know what, but for the first time in my life, I was looking for something.

Before the internet was very helpful for such things, my search brought me to a neighborhood bookstore, where I made my first big discovery. On a shelf for old books, I found a particularly handsome edition. In it, I read that the Bible contained a treasure of hidden secrets. This wisdom—not suitable for everybody—was supposedly encoded in the text. I was fascinated. Whether or not this was true, I wanted to know what this secret teaching was. The key to decoding the symbolic language was allegedly a mysterious system called the Kabbalah. I didn't know what it was, where to find it, or if it would really be what I wanted, but at least now I knew what I was looking for.

This old book that led me to Kabbalah was written by a freemason. Everything I'd heard about freemasons were extravagant stories of medieval knights, lost treasures, secret alliances, and political espionage. However, as I read, I found nothing like that. It was inspiring and dignified. The ideals it championed spoke to me. Principles of faith, tolerance, unconditional kindness, mutual support, and personal growth and improvement—qualities that benefit individuals and society in all times and places—are the foundation of masonic teaching. I thought that if this group was anything like it professed to be, I might like to be a part of it. This began my interest in Freemasonry. I learned as much as I could about its symbols and its hopelessly obscured and fragmented history. After years, I became a freemason myself.

I found my expectations of the group were only half right. My image of a well-disposed, amicable, even tight-knit order was confirmed. The sincere kindness and warm fellowship of the members is remarkable. Freemasons' commitments to each other, to their families, and to charity are as true as professed. However, Freemasonry was also supposed to be a storehouse of ancient wisdom. That part seemed to be missing. I didn't want to hear a secret word; I wanted to learn something. However, as I engaged with more members, I found only a few who shared my interest in symbolism or spirituality. Many more masons have little or no interest in either.

That brings me to the point of this book. First, I want to share with others a thing that has been so helpful to me: Kabbalah. The world of Kabbalah is unique, and the appeal for me was (and still is) not just its wonderful imagery but the amazing way those pictures are painted. More than assorted nuggets of wisdom, it's a creative, novel approach to understanding. This, I believe, makes Kabbalah a useful complement to Freemasonry. I'm not exaggerating when I call it my "spiritual key" to Freemasonry.

Second, I want to present a different image of Freemasonry—to the world at large, certainly, but also to masons themselves. As the public's perception of Freemasonry has deteriorated, the group's response has varied, with some turning increasingly inward and ignoring outside opinions, and others advocating for fundamental changes. I want to endorse a middle path, where Masonry maintains its friendly face *and* its reverent spirit along with its sincere heart and keen mind.

When I began writing this book, I imagined it would be useful for freemasons. As I continued, however, I thought it might actually appeal to anyone. Well, not exactly *anyone*. But anyone who seeks meaning in their life and all life, anyone searching for a way to relate to their neighbors rather than a reason not to, anyone interested in understanding and learning while still imagining and hoping—any of those people. This book might be for them. To all of them—all of you—freemason or otherwise, I hope you enjoy this book. I'm really happy I finally wrote it.

Since I was a child, I believed if something was true, one day, people would figure it out. Mostly, I still feel like that. In the same way earthly phenomena once thought to be supernatural have been demystified by a better understanding of nature, I believe the phenomena of human experience and consciousness may one day be as familiar and comprehensible as nightfall and thunderstorms. Still, existence is a mystery. Life is a mystery. The very world we live in is mysterious, and, thankfully, it always will be. Whatever answers we find are only answers to today's questions. There will always be new questions. Whenever we find out the new truth, we want to know the even greater truth that lies behind it. We want to know why it is and what else there could be. This is the grand quest of humanity—to know ourselves—and it goes on, still today, in earnest.

The actual history of Freemasonry may be impossibly lost. Despite many diligent efforts to discover the truth, little is known for sure about Freemasonry or any particular group of freemasons before their administration became more formalized in the early part of the eighteenth century. The oldest existing documents pertinent to Masonry are the so-called "Old Charges" that contain the rules and regulations of the medieval lodges of stoneworkers. Though certainly of great historical value to freemasons, the Old Charges are largely administrative documents and give little insight into the development of the modern symbolic tradition that eventually superseded the "operative" craft of stonework in the lodges altogether.

How long speculative practices have existed in Freemasonry and whether they were a late development is an interesting topic, but not my concern here. My hope is for this book to be practical. For this reason, it applies to Freemasonry now, in the first part of the twenty-first century, and as it might exist beyond that. So, while some background will at times be necessary to make a particular point, I've worried little about the "prehistory" of speculative Freemasonry. Many lengthy and rigorously investigated histories of Freemasonry have already been written. You shouldn't expect to find another one here.

Nor should you expect to find any suggestion of an age-old connection between Kabbalah and Freemasonry, nor the "real" meaning of Freemasonry's symbols, holy scripture, or anything else. This book is meant to help individuals locate personal meaning in symbols and rituals. It's a glimpse beyond mundane or unsatisfying explanations. This, I hope, will inspire you with a new or renewed appreciation of those symbols and, perhaps for the first time, give meaning to much of what may have seemed arbitrary. Even masons who aren't interested in "esoteric" topics will appreciate knowing a little bit more about the symbols. Those with a greater interest in symbolism will hopefully find what I've written welcome and satisfying.

I'd like to clarify the meaning of two words as they're used in the pages that follow: "esoteric" and "exoteric." *Esoteric* describes any fact, knowledge, or information a person must be "let in on" in order to know or understand. The esoteric meaning is always, by definition, the meaning shared by "insiders." Conversely, *exoteric* is the opposite. The exoteric explanation is plain to see; one presented to the general public. It is meant to be given to "outsiders." Today, freemasons use the term "esoteric" in two different ways. The first is to describe the "secret" content of their rituals. Certain aspects of masonic affairs, such as the solemn obligations, are to be kept private, while others, such as the masonic funeral ceremony, are shared with the public. The second way the word esoteric is used, refers to groups or practices where "higher" mystical explanations of Freemasonry's symbols, often spiritual or philosophical in nature, are sought or given.

This book contains ideas—my own ideas—that I hope will be helpful to you. I hope to encourage a greater understanding of symbolism more than a greater understanding of the symbols. Perhaps also, in a small way, Kabbalah will be rescued from the mass (or mess) of misconceptions that entangle it. Perhaps the same will be done for Freemasonry. Finally, for my fellow freemasons and every person reading this, I hope what I share improves your ability to provide meaning to your life. In the end, that is what I was after when I started this journey.

Peter Cardilla
Santa Cruz, CA
January 13, 2025

A Word on Translation

Translating any work, even a simple one, from one language to another is difficult. Because the *Zohar* is important to this book, it should be mentioned that translating the *Zohar* is a monumental undertaking far beyond my own capability or qualifications. The translations that I present in this work are predominantly those of the Pritzker edition published by Stanford University Press in twelve volumes (2003–2018), edited by Daniel Matt. The first nine volumes were translated by Matt himself, and the final three by Nathan Wolski and Joel Hecker. I have found this work indispensable to my study of the *Zohar*, and for the most part, it is this translation that I present throughout this book.

There are exceptions where I have preferred another translation, even if only for a particular phrase or specific word. In these cases (which I have indicated in the notes), the translations were taken from Isaiah Tishby's *Wisdom of the Zohar*, written originally in two volumes (1949, 1961), and translated from Hebrew into English by David Goldstein (1989).

Another text presented here is the *Shomer Emunim*, written by Joseph Ergas (1720) and published posthumously in Amsterdam in 1736. The translation I refer to here (2021), provided by Avinoam Fraenkel, is fantastic and provides English readers access to this excellent introduction to and explanation of the Kabbalah of Cordovero and Luria, which is for all intents and purposes the Kabbalah that has come down through history to today. Even here, however, the ultimate references are still almost always to the *Zohar*. The work of both Cordovero and Luria consists to a large degree in explaining and expanding on the concepts first presented in the "Holy" Zohar and in reinforcing its authenticity and authority.

All of these resources have been invaluable to my understanding, providing translation of the text with detailed and scholarly notation, particularly in their references to midrash and the Talmud. There are also a very few instances where I refer to Sperling and Simon's dated but at times usefully simple 1933 translation of the *Zohar*—the first into English. Where it is both relevant and expedient, I've explained my preference for an alternate translation.

In God I have put my trust. I will not fear what man can do unto me.

Psalms 56:11

PART 1

Introduction

And darkness was upon the face of the deep

The masonic journey is essentially the human journey. Because that journey is different for every person—whether they're a freemason or not—this book will be useful in different ways for every person. Masonry is a self-described "system of morality, veiled in allegory and illustrated by symbols."* This book is about interpreting symbols. However, more than simply sharing my interpretations (which I do) or those of others (which I also do), my greater hope is that you, the reader, will by the end of this book begin to discover your own interpretations of the symbols. Ones that have real meaning for you and perfectly align with your beliefs.

Many have heard of Freemasonry. A survey conducted by the Grand Lodge of California indicates nearly half that state's population is aware of the group's existence. If Freemasonry intended to be a "secret society," it didn't succeed. While public awareness of the "Honorable and Ancient Craft" is relatively high, the same survey reveals that public opinion of the group is rather low. Largely, the negative perception is undeserved. Popular beliefs that its members are part of a powerful elite or are involved in global conspiracies, for example, are based on rumors, gossip, and allegations that are simply untrue.† Ideas of this sort, resuscitated occasionally by popular books and movies, abide, for the most part, in

---

* This description is common and may first be attributable to William Preston.

† Much of the persistent misinformation about Freemasonry can be traced to nineteenth century French journalist Léo Taxil, who popularized fictitious accounts of a masonic conspiracy against the Pope. After years, he admitted the hoax, which did little to undo negative public perception.

1

works of fiction, and an increasingly sophisticated society now finds them more entertaining and less convincing.

More relevant—and more widely misunderstood—is Freemasonry's relationship with religion. As a requirement of admission, members must, even today, profess a personal belief in a "higher power" or "supreme being." Some believe this makes Masonry a religion of its own, a position the group itself disavows. Today, as more paths emerge and go in different directions, it becomes less clear what the word "religion" even means. For the purpose of this book, I define religion as the set of beliefs that describe your relationship with existence and reality. Not simply your understanding of space and matter, but the explanations you give to the experience of living. It's as much about why you believe it as it is about what you believe.

Rituals and moral prescriptions don't make a religion, they result from religion. Outward displays merely reflect the beliefs of the individual or group performing them. Some adhere to popular religions, others have an entirely personal religion. Your religion is everything you believe to be true about life, existence, and the world around you.

Formally, Masonry rejects the idea that it is a religion, but admits to being "religious." It retains a centuries-old practice of leaving its members to define their own spiritual and political beliefs.* In our ever more educated, secular, and religiously plural society, the discussion of religion has become increasingly fraught. Today, as in the past, Masonry's promotion of a "religion upon which all agree" allows diverse membership and avoids religious, political, and interpersonal controversy for the group and its members.

Freedom of religion, these days practically taken for granted in most Western countries, is still not a reality in an unfortunate number of places. In those places, religious controversy can be a genuinely serious matter and avoiding it is key to survival. Religious intolerance of this very dangerous type was the general rule, not the exception, in the embattled Europe that gave birth to Freemasonry. In England in

---

* There are irregular masonic groups with overt political associations.

1723, perhaps the only religious offense greater than subscribing to the "wrong" religion would have been to subscribe to no religion. Atheism would have been, for most, unthinkable, regarded as both illogical and immoral. Openly declaring a belief that there was no god would have brought serious consequences, legally and socially. For this reason, avoiding the question of religion altogether would not have been a practical option for the founders of modern Freemasonry, and was likely never a consideration. A religious element was, therefore, preserved but made as nonspecific as possible.

This faith requirement, intended originally to prevent religious controversy, in time became controversial itself. Politically motivated lodges in France (the discussion of politics is forbidden in regular masonic lodges) were among the earliest to question the required belief in a supreme being. Many voices inside and outside Masonry still question why, after three hundred years, there continues to be this requirement at all. This book offers fresh perspectives on belief and the place of "faith" in Masonry, ones that may make the answer clear to you or may change your perception of the matter entirely.

Conspiracy theorists and religious critics, however, are old problems for Masonry, and neither poses as great a threat as they once did. Today, the most damaging misconceptions of Freemasonry are those wherein the group is simply thought to be irrelevant, incompatible, or obsolete in contemporary society. This, it should be understood, is a relatively new problem for Freemasonry. Even during the height of political Anti-Masonry in the 1820s, Masonry was not lightly regarded. The group was opposed then, not because it was thought feckless but because it was believed to be too influential.

Beginning shortly after the First World War, Masonry experienced a membership boom that continued until its peak in the late 1950s. There were massive numbers on the rolls, with approximately 4 million American freemasons in 1959 representing more than 5 percent of the estimated adult male population at the time.* With that long-standing popularity came a steady accumulation of property and an investment in larger buildings, often in prime locations.

By the first half of the twentieth century, American Masonry was beginning to realize the financial burden of its now very valuable real estate holdings. Rather than increase dues on existing members, many groups began instead to implement policies aimed at increasing membership. From the measures taken, it appears Masonry's famous good-will and fellowship was identified as an attractive point to emphasize. The social activities of the group became the center of focus, and educational concerns moved to the periphery. However, bringing in new members would accomplish nothing if those members immediately left because advancement was too difficult or tedious. Other changes would also have to be made.

The Shriners, a masonic social order, soared in popularity in the early twentieth century.

---

* The number is based on an approximate US population of 177 million. Estimating the adult population to be between 65 and 78 percent of the general population, and 50 percent to be male, gives a number between 56 and 69 million. Four million masons would represent between 5 and 7 percent of adult American males in 1959.

Researcher Alex Towey, in reviewing the annual communications of the Grand Lodge of California, summarizes, "It is apparent that in 1920 we can see the rise of social Freemasonry and the decline of educational Freemasonry." This change, though issued from the top, reflected trends present within the broader membership. Towey shows grave concern was expressed by high ranking masons at the time about the deliberate shift away from education to a focus on socializing.

As early as 1918, California's masonic leadership recognized that "By failing to respond to the intellectual and spiritual demands of their members some of our lodges are losing the interest and active support of many of the best masons . . . and are in danger of becoming the patrons of the mediocre."[1] Again in 1920, there was concern over the "ill-fate of lodges if not given importance to ritual and philosophy."[2] In the records from that same year, the opinion was recorded that there were "too many members and not enough masons."[3] In 1923, the Grand Lecturer of California remarked the ritual was often performed without being explained or even understood by those presenting it.[4]

The situation was not isolated to California. Among the most prominent masonic authors of the time, W. L. Wilmshurst addressed both sides of the issue in 1924. He wrote the "educative work has been grievously neglected" and "some members have no wish to be masonically educated."[5] He also points out the damage this was causing to Freemasonry as an institution: "In every lodge are [found] earnest seekers of Wisdom and Light [who] lose interest when their needs are left unprovided for."[6]

The warnings of those who opposed the degradation of masonic education would soon seem prophetic. The movement away from education occurred not just in California but across many, if not all, masonic jurisdictions.[7] Through the 1950s membership had been stable and, except for a couple years during the Great Depression, growing for decades. The institution, expecting further growth and having only known popularity, did not anticipate what happened next. Beginning in the 1960s there was a noticeable decline in both the membership of the group and its public visibility. This decline has continued into the beginning of the twenty-first century.

Initially Freemasonry, perhaps not wanting to overreact and certainly unsure of what to do, had little response. By the 1980s, with the negative trend still unabated, it perhaps should have been clear the efforts intended to raise membership in the 1920s were not working. However, unable to determine or agree about the underlying reasons for their declining popularity, many lodges and grand lodges continued and even expanded these policies. Campaigns aimed at increasing membership were launched, as before, with the mixed support of the existing members. Few initiatives, if any, had a noticeable positive effect. Membership continued to decline as it had been while much of the response remained focused on "making it easier" for people to join and become active in lodge administration. Reducing what was expected of members, however, did not increase outside interest in the group. The problem was—and is—something different.

So what happened? Society was changing, especially in its attitudes toward religion and education. Organized religion was declining in popularity. An emphasis on the value of education, particularly college and university education, was growing. Across all social organizations, not just Freemasonry, participation dropped. The shift in Western culture away from its former values left Masonry as part of the "old guard" where it has largely remained, even until today. As masonic author Christopher Hodapp noted in a 2019 article, Masonry's superannuated style can appear strange even to its own members:[8]

> Those pre-1960s generations were not put off by what many today see as tortured language in the rituals . . . What many modern masons see as creaky or anachronistic stage plays . . . were common currency up to three generations ago, when your next-door neighbors were still actively involved in local theater groups, and every teenager learned debating and speech making.

In a future-facing world, Freemasonry was, generally speaking, old-fashioned. Specifically difficult to overlook in a society eager to distance itself from its religious past, were the outward appearance of many of

Freemasonry's symbols. Much of the group's form is retained from the time of its inception and reflects the world into which it was born. Signs of the dominant forces of that era, specifically European monarchs and the Christian church, are obvious still today. Since the 1960s, however, both church and state have come to be viewed (especially by young Westerners) with a certain amount of suspicion. Freemasonry, being both religious and patriotic and offering no voice in its own public defense, had little hope of faring well. In some ways, it bore a dual fate: condemned as too religious by some and as too secular or even heretical by others.

Along with society's new view of Masonry, Masonry's view of itself had changed, shifting away from a philosophical focus to a social one. Over generations, the pattern of gradually de-prioritizing "ritual and philosophy," identified by Wilmshurst and others, had the predictable effect. By the 1960s, generations of masons had received the degrees of Freemasonry with little elaboration on the meaning of the symbols and ritual. Discussion of symbolism was reduced to the simplest explanations. Today, the ability to explain Masonry's symbols, including its ritual—the entirety of which is symbolic—has been significantly lost. Worse perhaps, it's so long been looked upon as obsolete and valueless that, today, many masons have no serious regard for the symbolism.

It is safe to say that Freemasonry does not sit in the same position it once did in our towns and communities. Masonry's old-fashioned and Christian persona—and inability to explain itself in another way—has for years disengaged a growing portion of the public. Unsuccessful efforts to reverse declines in membership by de-emphasizing education left the group not only with a much smaller membership, but one that has little knowledge or interest regarding the symbols. This is the state of Masonry today.

The use of symbolism is a defining characteristic of Freemasonry, so I was surprised when I first realized that remarkably few masons are terribly concerned with it. Perhaps I shouldn't have been. This has likely always been the case. The fact that the changes in the early twentieth century were adopted and maintained for generations, despite the warnings of Masonry's most distinguished voices, suggests care for the symbols was not particularly widespread among masons. While the ritual may have once been more carefully practiced, the current idea among some groups within Masonry today—that symbolism was once more widely understood by freemasons than it is now—is likely a misconception. There's no evidence that there was ever a particularly widespread interest in esoteric discussions of symbolism, or philosophy in general. This aspect of Masonry has probably always, for as long as it's existed, been maintained by a few. The perception that "the masons of old" had a "greater" or "deeper" relationship with the symbols and ritual is probably explainable by considering two factors.

First, Western society was much more religious in the seventeenth and eighteenth centuries than it is now. All freemasons of the time, many with no interest in esoteric ideas, are likely to have taken a greater and more personal satisfaction from the plain, exoteric explanations. They didn't necessarily "dig deeper" or feel a value in doing so. The plain meaning spoke directly to their religious beliefs. Second, those who might have had a greater interest in esoterica came into Masonry with a basic education far better suited to the interpretation of symbols than what a typical education provides today. Their familiarity with the Bible, classical mythology, the Greek and Latin languages, European folklore, and history are qualities they likely brought to the fraternity, and not something they gained from it. While a typical high school graduate today may learn more about chemistry than what Isaac Newton knew (oxygen had not yet been discovered in Newton's time), they probably can't quote from scripture or poetry, read and write in Latin, recognize allusions to classic literature, or discuss the symbolism of the Greek pantheon. All of which were done as matters of course for Newton and many of his contemporaries, and all of which would inform their interpretation of symbols.

Today, many of those interests are categorically abandoned. Religion and mythology are not seen as pertaining to philosophy or ethics. They are, to the contrary, roundly dismissed as superstition and magic.

Classic literature and folk traditions are regarded as a glimpse only into the obsolete ideas of an immoral, unethical, and uninformed "dark-age" from which little can or should be learned. The loss of what was formerly considered wisdom is hardly perceived to be a deficit, and is even celebrated by many as liberation from past ignorance. Over time, disregard leads to neglect. In this case, the symbols of the past have been collectively cast to the dustheap.

Despite some alarming predictions, there is a chance all is not lost. After sixty years of steadily declining membership, there may be signs of hope for Freemasonry. Beginning in the early 2000s, some masonic jurisdictions noticed the loss in membership slowing for the first time in years and the number of new members actually increasing. Importantly, the new membership seems to have an expressed interest in masonic education. In 2010, it had become the opinion of California's masonic leadership that "the membership and new members want masonic education and a greater membership experience."[9] However, for those masons, the ones who seek this education and greater experience, new problems now exist.

First, almost a hundred years of negligence has had a noticeable effect. Most masons today haven't been taught anything more about the symbols than what is provided in the plain presentation of their ceremonies. Perhaps it's to be expected that those same masons can, therefore, give no greater explanation of them to others. Second, shortened ceremonies and reduced requirements exacerbated the problem, allowing masons to selectively avoid teaching or learning some of the symbols altogether. Finally, changes in modern secular education, especially since the middle of the twentieth century, produced students who, compared to previous generations, were less inclined to the interpretation of symbols. While Freemasonry remains rich in possession of symbols, the fact that many of them are not well understood, is unfortunate. The symbols of Freemasonry should teach and inspire. Obviously, symbols without meaning fall short of both aims.

To be clear, I don't share the concern of some others, that the "true" or "original" meaning of the symbols has been, or will be, lost to time or that it hasn't been carefully preserved. To have that concern would suggest I believe a symbol has a "true" meaning. I do not. Symbols are interpreted to have meaning. What has been lost, or at least what has not been well preserved, is the practice of seeing and finding meaning in a symbol. Those of you who are helped and encouraged by this book to interpret the symbols for yourselves will be, I have no doubt, inspired by the new world you find.

Masonry's future place in our or any community can't be taken for granted. Any who believe Masonry has a right to exist without question are ignoring the facts of the present and forgetting the lessons of the past. American Masonry was seriously endangered by a political attack in the 1820s and all but entirely forsaken following social change in the 1960s. Even in the twenty-first century, Freemasonry is strictly forbidden by law in several countries around the world and outlawed by the Roman Catholic Church. The many symbols and rich traditions of Freemasonry could still, after all these years, be lost. Its preservation will only come from the efforts of those who concern themselves with it. To those, I

Pope Clement XII (left) issued a papal bull in 1738 outlawing Freemasonry.
Nearly 300 years later in 2023, Pope Francis (right) reaffirmed the Catholic ban.

suggest looking to Kabbalah as a well-suited example for Freemasonry to follow and one worthy of imitation.

Kabbalah is therefore presented here, not as a curriculum, with facts to learn and correspondences to memorize, but as a model for how Freemasonry can and, if it's going to survive into the future, how in some ways it must be. If you are familiar with Kabbalah and are surprised by the presentation I make of it, I hold out hope that in the end your surprise will be pleasant. Similarities and parallels pointed out between Kabbalah and Freemasonry, are in no way meant to show or suggest a past relationship. They're intended to illustrate details common between the situation that Kabbalah faced and, by many measures, successfully navigated nearly a thousand years ago, and the one that Masonry is currently in the midst of, and—if the most dismal current projections are accurate—in which it seems to be hopelessly adrift.[10]

Teach a man to fish

Most have heard the expression that advises "Give a man a fish and he'll eat for a day. Teach a man to fish and he'll eat for a lifetime." Even if you've never heard it before, the meaning is not hard to figure out. In the long run, a person benefits more from knowing how to do a thing for themselves than they do from having someone do it for them. This is certainly true. It is also true, that the proverbial "teacher" in the situation benefits as well from the other person's self-improvement because they no longer have the burden of providing for them. So the newly-taught fisherperson benefits with less dependency on others, and the teacher benefits with less demand on them. However, there is another possible benefit to this exchange. When a person is taught to fish, there is a chance that they will become better at fishing than the person teaching them! They may become the best fisher that ever lived, and catch fish that have never been seen before, and benefit the whole community. Teaching a person to fish doesn't just make them self-reliant—it increases the chances for the world to improve.

By teaching masons how to symbolically fish, not only will they become less reliant on explanations from others—explanations that may never be forthcoming—they will also, when the time comes, be better *givers* of fish themselves. As earnest and diligent as any person might be in teaching another, it's normal that things take time to develop for the student. In fact, it's often the case at first that the new fisher still needs help until they become self-sufficient and your fish-giving days are not yet behind you. There are also those who have never fished before. If your fish don't look appealing to them, they aren't likely to follow your example. However, if they see you catching beautiful and delicious fish, you may create a fisher for life. One day they might become so skilled they teach you how to fish in even deeper, richer, or faster-flowing waters.

Telling a mason what a symbol means is like giving a person a fish. If your explanation isn't very good, that person won't be satisfied and might be left with a bad taste in their mouth. This describes the experience of a significant number of contemporary masons who are expecting more than they end up receiving in terms of explanation or instruction. As a result, some feel disillusioned and discouraged. If, on the other hand, a person is satisfied with what they receive, they will seek more. Eventually, however, the problem becomes that the student needs something the teacher can't give. Sooner or later, you'll have to teach them to fish for themselves. Even after telling someone everything you know, at a certain point they ask questions that you never asked and need answers that you've never found. Teach a mason how to find their own meanings in the symbols and that mason will find those answers, and in the future be able to teach others.

As a mason is introduced to Kabbalah, the symbols of Freemasonry start to appear in a different light. Kabbalah both *gives* fish, and *teaches* a mason to fish. That is, a certain amount of familiarity with the symbolic language is prerequisite for understanding Kabbalah. Learning the special vocabulary of kabbalists, symbols known as the *sephirot*, any mason is likely to notice a broad correspondence between the terminology of Kabbalah and Masonry. Understanding the meaning of these terms as they relate to Kabbalah, gives a different perspective by which to appreciate them as masonic symbols. These are the *fish* which Kabbalah gives at first. In addition, Kabbalah consists of a number of interpretive techniques that are applied to the scripture of the Hebrew Bible, and by which are extracted the most wonderful and unexpected meanings from verses. By employing Kabbalah's techniques to discover personal meaning in the symbols, language, and ritual of Masonry, as well as everyday life, you also learn *how to fish*.

There is a significant overlap of symbols between Kabbalah and Masonry which is largely, but I wouldn't say entirely, coincidental. However, despite the intriguing hints of a shared past, what makes Kabbalah relevant to Freemasonry today is its true origin. The forces that came to bear on Judaism almost a thousand years ago, and which gave birth to Kabbalah, are in some ways analogous to those that were in place in Britain during the Enlightenment, where modern Masonry was born. Similar forces exist again in contemporary Western culture, against which modern Masonry strives valiantly for its own survival. Kabbalah is, in many ways, the product of a conflict between the comfort and stability afforded by tradition and the critical recommendations of rational thinking. In the twelfth century, rational Jewish philosophy challenged the mythology of popular Judaism. This challenge foreshadowed one made later by "natural philosophy" to the backwards but still powerful, religious governments of seventeenth and eighteenth century Europe. A similar tension again appears in the contemporary challenge of secularism to the spiritual remnant in the West.

It's not so simple

Both Freemasonry and Kabbalah have long been mediators in what is often categorized today as a conflict between "science and religion." This so-called conflict is really only the latest skirmish in an age-old war waged within the consciences of people and societies, pitting *reason* and *ethics* against what ancient Greeks called *passion* and *appetite*. Often lost sight of today, is the fact that up until somewhat recently, the modern distinction between science and religion did not exist. In fact, real differences between any fields of inquiry were, for most of history, in no way clear. From ancient times until the nineteenth century, nearly everything that is now called *science* was encompassed by the term *natural philosophy*.

Philosophers, of all sorts as they were, tried to understand and explain both the physical world around them and the internally experienced world of the mind. They tried to understand the physiology of humans and animals. They imagined the beginning of time and searched for the building blocks of all matter. They tried to understand how the whole world and everything in it was created from nothing and wondered what *nothing* would even be like. All of these pursuits are ongoing. The names and finer details of the practices have changed, but the nature of the questions we are asking are still the same. How does the world work? What is the human experience in the world? How does everything fit together? We still haven't found all the answers.

Of course, today we know a lot more about the questions we're asking than we used to. The amount of knowledge we have acquired in every area of science is massive. Science and learning are now greatly specialized pursuits. A significant advance in any field of modern science or philosophy is likely to require a lifetime of effort, including general and specialized education, research, analysis, and a few strokes of good fortune along the way. The legendary polymaths of the past, experts across multiple domains, are largely relegated to stay there: in the past. Every modern field of study simply contains too much for a single person to be expert in multiple fields. Individuals tend to have specific areas of expertise—very talented ones may have two or three—and perhaps a small handful of additional pursuits in which they're particularly competent. But the world we live in is complicated. People often (in fact, everybody, every day) require or rely on the specific knowledge of

Gottfried Wilhelm Leibnitz, credited alongside Isaac Newton, with inventing calculus. Considered to be among the last great polymaths.

others that is beyond our own. When it happens that questions arise in those areas, we are forced to rely on experts in those fields.

Except, for some reason, we seem not to like to do that. Sometimes we do it, but certainly not as much as we should. When things are important, usually in matters of immediate life and death, it's been observed that people tend to be efficient, cooperative, and able to rely on their training.[11] However, outside of extreme circumstances we're all subject to prejudices and predispositions, which normally impose themselves on our decision making. We play favorites. We hold grudges. We seek revenge and vindication. We decide beforehand what is true and what is nonsense, what is good and what is bad, what is right and what is wrong, and we focus too much on some information and exclude other information entirely. This affects what questions we ask, what sources we trust, and what messages we listen to, as well as what questions we *don't* ask, what sources we *don't* trust, and what messages we *don't* listen to.

Knowing our biases can be helpful in mitigating their impact. If we consider that we may have allowed a preconceived idea to wrongly cloud our judgment, we might be able to correct ourselves. But still, we might not. Concepts like "confirmation bias" and "in-group/out-group bias" are not new or little understood ideas in psychology, but knowing about them doesn't mean you're immune to their effects. Cognitive biases aren't always clear to the person experiencing them. Additionally, some people believe certain prejudices to be examples of virtue, and, in those cases, extreme displays of prejudice might be showcased as exalted virtue. Uncritical thinking, however, should never be celebrated. It's no true virtue to dismiss something categorically and unexamined. These types of biases underlie the modern false dichotomy between science and religion.

For most of Western history, *all* scientific advances were made by religious people in religious societies. The very concept of being "non-religious" would have seemed nonsensical and atheism would have been regarded as an insanity tantamount to denying reality. It's not until the seventeenth century that the concept of "religiousness" started to take shape as increased travel introduced European cultures to different and previously unknown spiritual traditions. The term "science" emerged later, in the nineteenth century, as different approaches to the study of nature began to require specification. By the twentieth century, the difference was starting to become more stark in the public perception. Science was tomorrow, religion was yesterday. Science was space-age, religion was stone-age. Science was progressive, religion was repressive, if not oppressive. Science promised everything we wanted, religion threatened everything we feared. In short, science was good and getting better and religion was bad and getting worse.

The idea that a conflict exists between science and religion, the so-called "conflict paradigm" has gained traction in our culture. It suggests an inherent incompatibility separating the two. Those who have this belief tend to view others as either religious or scientific, but not both. Of course, the truth is not that simple. This is not how people see themselves and, more importantly, it's not supported by data. A recent study reveals that scientists across both natural and social sciences do not view science and religion as incongruent. Interestingly, the conflict paradigm was held to be true mostly among those scientists who, compared to their peers, had the least immediate knowledge of religion.[12]

In actuality, there are no such things as religious people or scientific people. There are religious beliefs and scientific beliefs; and everybody has both. People with every variety of religious beliefs rely on science. On the other hand, "science people," even the most devout atheist among them, still have religious beliefs. They may be very unusual, unorthodox, and entirely personal beliefs, but if they concern the nature of truth or reality, and are believed despite the fact that they can't be tested or proven, those are religious beliefs. Before deciding that you are a pure rationalist and have no religion, ask yourself: do I believe in concepts such as human rights, or the value of life, or right and wrong, or good and bad? Any of those are religious beliefs. Whether or not people have rights is not a matter of science. It is generally a matter of politics. The government defines and protects the rights of the citizens. However, the idea that humans have certain "rights" that occur so naturally, that the government cannot justifiably take them away—so-called human rights—is a religious belief. There is no way to scientifically test or prove this idea. If you believe this is true, you just do.

The value of faith

"I know that I know nothing." This statement, attributed to Socrates, reflects the idea that many times what a person calls *knowledge* would better be called *belief*. This position—we don't really know what we think we know—is neither natural nor comfortable, and continues to be provocative thousands of years after the words were written. People are quite confident in their knowledge, particularly where their identities are tied to it. We rely on our knowledge to survive—our training, our experience—we don't just *believe* these things, we *know* them. The difference between these things we claim to "know" and those which we profess only to "believe" is, in the end, the degree of doubt versus certainty.

This was Socrates's point, and one that is contained in the lessons of Freemasonry. The things we say we *know* are those things we *believe* to be true with absolute certainty. We know our own names. We know the town we grew up in. We *know* these things, we have no doubt about them at all. Conversely, when we say we believe something, it implies that there is some doubt. We *believe* the favorite will win the race, but that doesn't always happen. Statistically speaking it should, and it normally will, but there is no guarantee and sometimes the long shot wins.

It might take some convincing

It's the degree of certainty that separates what we think of as *knowledge* from our other beliefs. We say of ourselves that we know a thing *for certain* and *beyond the shadow of a doubt*. But where does this certainty come from? How can a person be certain about anything? What convinces a person beyond doubt? Humans generally have a reason for the things we believe. A person weighs evidence and decides if it's convincing. Evidence that convinces one person does not convince everybody. Even among members of a group who essentially see and experience the same things, a large variety of opinions exist. The simple fact is, the details some find irrefutable and pertinent, others find irrelevant and nonsensical. Therefore, one person "knows" with certainty the same thing another only somewhat believes, a third doubts with great skepticism, and a fourth refutes as impossible. All four people may have heard the same evidence and understood it the same way, but they were convinced by it to differing degrees. The one who believes it completely, is convinced they *know* it.

Well, what makes you so sure?

Some reasons we feel certainty are obvious. We are convinced by logic and reasoning. When we are seeking an explanation, it usually goes without saying that we are seeking a *logical* explanation. Additionally, we are convinced by what we see with our own eyes or hear with our own ears. That is, *seeing is believing. I'll believe it when I see it*, an old expression confesses. Humans trust our senses implicitly and this, notes philosopher Charles Peirce, is our earliest act of faith.[13]

The belief that the images formed by our brains, after interpreting the data gathered by our senses, accurately represent the external reality, *is* an act of faith. We don't see a dog; we see the light that reflects off of the dog. But we don't really see the light either. The light waves enter our eyes and that information is conveyed to the brain electrically. What we "see," after the original information has undergone these several processes, is an image produced by our mind. We have faith that image is an accurate reflection of the real world. However, we "see" images in our "mind's eye" when we dream too. These often "look" exactly like the images we "see" when we're awake, but most people don't *believe* that they represent reality.

Along with the five senses, the *sense* of logic or what some call human reasoning, is also very convincing. People, in general, are very confident about their own powers of logical deduction. However, human reasoning is often unreliable to this end. The problem is despite what we traditionally or naturally think, the facts are becoming more clear; human reasoning is not necessarily or automatically *logical*. Current science suggests that logic plays a smaller part in human reason than was once believed.[14] Research is demonstrating empirically something that many have observed for a long time; human reasoning arrives at conclusions which are, very often, illogical. Unsurprising as that may be, the word has been slow to get out. People still overestimate not just their own logical ability, but that of humans in general.

To point out the limits of human senses and logic is not to discount or speak against the importance of either one. Masonry teaches and promotes both as fundamental to its practice. Learning by direct use of the senses—that is, by observable phenomena—and applying a logical and reasoned approach to life, are essential to masonic teaching. However, it is important to understand the limits of human perception and reasoning, and to accept them. Accepting that human wisdom is limited, particularly our own, makes it possible to appreciate different opinions. As masonic scholar Rex Hutchens wrote: "[fundamentalists] carved out of faith, certainty; out of certainty, intolerance; out of intolerance, infallibility; and out of infallibility; persecution."[15]

Having some doubt is, generally speaking, a good thing. Being open to the possibility that you might be wrong, is a sign of humility and a crucial requirement of science and critical thinking. Being humble is not, as some understand, thinking poorly about yourself, or esteeming others above you. It is being honest in your assessment of yourself and others. Humility isn't to inflate others insincerely or to criticize yourself unfairly. It gives credit where due and takes credit only where earned.

Humility aside, it's not practical to doubt *everything*. At some point a person has to be able to believe what they see, hear, and touch. We *have to* trust our senses or the world becomes unimaginably frightening and dangerous. This trust, as Peirce pointed out, is, in the end, a matter of faith. People move through life confident that the world as they see it around them is the world as it actually exists, but some uncertainty must remain. Is the world we see, hear, and feel *really* the world that is? Honestly we may never know. This small but undeniable uncertainty maintains belief as faith and stops it from becoming the inflexible certitude of the zealot and the bigot, two sworn enemies of Freemasonry.

Finally, as will be further discussed, faith completes the idea of charity and begays hope. The earnest belief that it *will* have its desired effect not only motivates charity, it legitimizes it. Generosity, if extended with no belief that it will be helpful, is strangely motivated and not charity. Hope, without belief that it will happen, is eventually abandoned. It becomes a memory of something once sincerely desired, but no longer brings with it a feeling of hopefulness. On the other hand, hope with faith is expectant, like a child looking forward to their birthday party. Faith—believing what *can* happen, *will* happen—converts hope from longing to anticipation. So masons maintain the charitable idea that life should be better, hope that it can be better and faith that it will be better.

So here we go

Contemporary society requires Freemasonry to make room for an increasingly diverse membership, with religious ideas that differ widely, from the secular spiritualist to the devout and orthodox. Kabbalah's value to Masonry is the way it speaks to all spiritual paths. Though its own roots are in Jewish tradition, its message—once decoded—is universal. The faithful of all religions, the spiritual on any path, and the seeker of every sort, can readily identify with the concepts found in Kabbalah as compatible with their own.

Kabbalah deals almost entirely with interpreting the Hebrew Bible, better known to many as the Old Testament. This is also the predominant source of Freemasonry's symbols. For those symbols, Kabbalah adds a richness to their understanding, and the payoff is immediate. Though the Bible is relatively well known to many, especially among masons, Kabbalah's highly unique presentation makes reading it quite different than most have ever imagined. Even the most familiar verses are experienced like they're brand new. Made over in the symbols of Kabbalah, the most mundane scripture is reborn as a dynamic tale, and the most well-trodden paths are, again and always, fresh adventures.

Referred to as it has been up to now, Kabbalah may seem to be, as is often mistakenly assumed, a single, well-defined and coherent program. Such a misconception, though common, is far from the truth. The definition of Kabbalah is only loosely agreed upon, if at all. Its written works have no official canon and consist of a handful of major writings and countless smaller—less well-known, but not always less important—published works and manuscripts. Agreement between sources is, even in the best cases, partial, and almost nothing is said in one place that isn't seemingly contradicted in another.

The unpolished details and minor inconsistencies, however, end up being of little consequence. The system that emerges has no need for the type of doctrinal precision that is required of religious dogma. Kabbalah is, in the end, neither a science nor a religion but a contemplative practice more akin to art than to true philosophy. There is no fact of matter, event in history, or royal authority that Kabbalah must defend. Kabbalah isn't trying to prove anything mathematically or assert its own authority over and above orthodox leadership, so an occasionally unresolved detail is simply and easily excused or overlooked. To focus too much on minor inconsistencies or any technical details of Kabbalah is, anyway, to miss the point.

Masons who are reading this may already sense vague similarities between Kabbalah and Freemasonry. Masonry is, in the same way, often thought and spoken of as a single coherent movement. Similarly, it is not. The "landmarks" and defining characteristics of Freemasonry are not universally agreed upon. There is no single "official" ritual for all jurisdictions or bodies and between them there is wide disagreement in that regard. Its symbols and mythology have demonstrably changed over time. Any of these issues, however, is beside the point. Despite all this, it is not vacuous and unidentifiable. Freemasonry is still *something*. It's recognizable by its symbols and by its fundamental ideals. The same is true of Kabbalah.

Between Freemasonry and Kabbalah the greatest similarity—and the one which ultimately binds them—is that they are both symbolic systems. Along with its symbols, the techniques of Kabbalah and its liberated, unorthodox approach to symbolism, are wonderful tools for masons looking for deeper or more personal meaning in their own symbols. The symbolic system of Freemasonry teaches moral lessons and it's aimed at developing and promoting virtue. Underlying this, there is an undeniable spiritual aspect that directs Masonry's course and motivates its activity. Even appropriately understated as it is, the religious element is not invisible. Because of this, masons who don't consider themselves to be religious, can be unsure about how to receive such symbols and

Sign outside masonic lodge in Rehovot, Israel. It reads, "Hall of Freemasons, Bilu Lodge No. 33

traditions, and may instead choose to avoid them. Kabbalah, in its own way, reflects rational philosophic ideas, in a religiously satisfying form. Masons who have chosen to disregard or avoid certain symbols, may, after reading this book, be encouraged to re-approach them, and might find meaning in them after all.

Today there is a healthy interest in Kabbalah, among masons and within other Western spiritual and contemplative traditions. It's also true that many who are interested, particularly masons, have no idea where to even start. The uncurated internet is, in many cases, worse than no help. Likely to be found there is a very confusing mess of many different things, all of which are being called Kabbalah.* A large number of books exist, many of them excellent, but without some guidance a novice is unlikely to find the right one before reading several others which were *not* right.

This book is meant to be a starting point, of course for all freemasons, but especially for those with an interest in the symbols, and perhaps as well for any person with an earnest interest in Kabbalah or Freemasonry. Those hoping to find an exposure of masonic secrets, or a story of Masonry's long-lost ties to Kabbalah, will not find that here. This is a

---

* or Cabala or Qabbala or another variant spelling.

book about ideas and how they are connected to—and connect—the world we live in. It's about the ideas we all have in common and how to recognize them, and how those ideas simultaneously reflect and shape reality. Winding through history, science, philosophy, and religion, what follows is, I believe, a novel approach to considering those ideas; the ideas that form the necessary first step in Masonry, Kabbalah, and every journey of discovery. Hence, the Beginning is Wisdom.

CHAPTER 1

Freemasonry, Kabbalah, and Symbolism

Masonry is important

Freemasonry, often just called Masonry, is among the largest and oldest membership organizations in the world today. Shrouded in secrecy for years and the subject of countless conspiracy theories, Masonry has classically described itself as a "system of morality, veiled in allegory and illustrated by symbols." This is a fine description of the group, but it hardly makes clear what freemasons do. When asked about Masonry, my usual response is to say that Freemasonry is three things. First, it is a fraternity. The members look out for and take care of each other. Second, it is a charitable organization supporting schools, libraries, and hospitals around the world with millions of dollars donated annually to initiatives aimed at public education, literacy, and children's health. And finally, Masonry promotes self-improvement, encouraging each member to focus on becoming a better person.

Freemasonry is important. Not because its membership has famously included some of the most influential people in history, but because of what it has offered to society wherever it's flourished. In the often tumultuous ideological shift from the faith and fealty of the past to modern logic and scientific reason, Freemasonry provided a safe place for the open exchange of ideas. This change continues to take place around the world still today. Across much of Europe, it occurred following the Middle

Ages,* when the dangers of religious and political intolerance were often extreme. Freemasonry emerged in the centuries which followed as a decidedly non-controversial group of gentlemen; charitable and social, religious and ethical.

Taking its modern form during the European Enlightenment of the seventeenth and eighteenth centuries, Freemasonry legendarily grew out of trade guilds that had flourished through all parts of the Roman Empire since early antiquity. Throughout the Middle Ages, guilds provided technical training, job placement, wage security, and insurance for their members and their families. Lodges, set up onsite, often for years during massive construction projects, would be where the workmen slept, ate, and received instruction.

Gerhard von Rile, also known as Meister Gerhard, was the first master mason in charge of the construction of the Cologne Cathedral in 1248.

However, by the beginning of the Modern era at the end of the fifteenth century, the usefulness of the guild lodges was diminishing. New laws and labor organizations began to provide the same professional benefits. At some point, it becomes clear that lodges of stonemasons began to admit members who were not actually workers in stone or any trade for that matter, including nobility and men of letters. The scant surviving record of the practice, apparently called the "acception," leaves its origin and purpose unknown. What is known is that by the final decades of the seventeenth century, the membership of these lodges bore an increasing

---

* The Middle Ages, or Medieval era, is roughly delineated from the fifth to fifteenth centuries CE.

number of "gentleman" masons and a shrinking number of "operatives," as the stoneworkers came to be called.

During this period, in the early 1600s, a series of brutal religious and civil wars across Europe had destroyed the already strained relationship between Catholics and Protestants. The Thirty Years' War between German Protestant states and the powerful Catholic Habsburg monarchy was the bloodiest in European history. It resulted in a humiliating defeat for the Protestants. Enflamed by the war and encouraged by their victory in it, the Catholic-ruled countries of Europe saw a resurgence in witch hunts and the violent persecution of magic, heresy, and secret societies. In Britain, this unrest was followed almost immediately by their own series of costly civil wars, also largely delineated between Protestants and Catholics, often pitting England against neighboring Scotland. These wars split the allegiance of the people between two royal families and two religions.

Amid this atmosphere of unrest and intrigue, Freemasonry took its modern form in England and Scotland. The years of bloody conflict, betrayal, and mistrust still affected the public conscience. Despite this, the era remains known to history for advancing the more positive developments of the preceding centuries. The so-called Scientific Revolution, which began during the Renaissance, produced advances in learning that set the foundation for modern society. During the Enlightenment, ideals of science and reason, natural law, and the value of personal liberty and religious tolerance, were popular. Learned societies, such as the Royal Society of London, became well regarded, as much for their amazing demonstrations of science and nature as for the nobility and high character of their members, patrons, and guests.

Led primarily by their gentleman membership, many of whom were fellows and some of whom were founders of the Royal Society, four London lodges came together in 1717 with an agreement to form the first grand lodge. Within a few years, the Premiere Grand Lodge held its first convention and introduced the new rules and regulations for the group, which they called *the Constitutions*. The individuals who crafted these founding documents, in doing so, borrowed from texts called *the Old Charges*. This collection of manuscripts, some dating back to the late fourteenth century, contained the regulations and procedures of the medieval stonemasons.

Though the new documents resembled the style and form of the old charges, contemporary thought, reflecting the values of the Enlightenment, had been superimposed onto the "ancient" framework. One example is the original requirement for members to believe in a Christian Trinitarian god, being reborn in the "New Charges" as an obligation to "that Religion in which all Men agree." Masonry, inspired by the progressive spirit of the era, made itself (as it remains today) open to those of every religion, race, and creed. Considering the tense political and religious climate of the time, this approach allowed for diverse membership, without forcing individuals to openly identify their religion, potentially exposing themselves to personal or professional danger.

Masonry today

Freemasonry today, with membership universally in decline, finds itself in a possible existential crisis. An increasingly sophisticated society has left traditional ideas of god and religion largely in the past. The typical person is no longer satisfied with supernatural or magical explanations for their questions. They rely on reason and observation. It is not uncommon to hear people today describe themselves as "spiritual but not religious." This is usually meant to indicate that they have a sense of something greater than themselves, but reject the formal teachings of organized religions. A growing number of masons fall into this category. These members often have difficulty finding real meaning in the large amount of Freemasonry's symbolism taken from Judeo-Christian sources, specifically the Bible.

The leaders of Freemasonry, the keepers of its heritage and stewards of its future, have now the work of integrating contemporary ideas into their centuries-old traditions. Many understand why traditions are important and believe they should be preserved when it's possible and prudent. Traditions connect people to each other in the present, past, and future. Physicist Brian Greene recalls a powerful example in his book, *Until the End of Time*, when he was struck by the difference between imagining he only had twenty-four hours to live and imagining the whole world would be destroyed in twenty-four hours. It's one thing to imagine that you won't be here tomorrow. It's another thing to imagine that nothing will. Our life in the present is given meaning, in part, by our hope for the future. As children we imagine ourselves as adults. Once we're grown, we work with an eye toward promotion, then retirement. At the end of our lives we think about posterity, our children and grandchildren, our legacy. Even though we won't be around to see it, and have no idea what it holds, for many of us it's important to believe that some future exists.

We also want to have a connection to the past. It's important to have roots, to be part of a lineage, to be the continuation of something spanning generations and lifetimes. If the future gives us something to hope for, the past gives us something to be accountable to. People want to preserve the "good name" they inherited from their family, to live up to its legacy. They are proud alumni of the school they attended. They observe holidays, share folklore, and honor memorials. Traditions are inherited from the past and bequeathed to the future and they connect us to each other along the way.

The tradition Masonry has been given, and which it now must preserve and pass on, consists of its symbols and ritual. An inheritance of icons and ceremonies into which a rich treasure of moral and spiritual meaning have been woven. To maintain tradition and carry it forward into the modern world, Freemasonry must restore in itself the practice of interpreting and contemplating its symbols. A symbol means only as little or every bit as much as it means to the person interpreting it, whatever that may be. Understanding and making use of masonic symbolism is not a matter of learning what symbols mean, but rather learning how to interpret meaning from them. Kabbalah embodies this approach exceptionally well.

Kabbalah

To understand how it can and does relate to Freemasonry, it helps to know what Kabbalah is and where it came from. Kabbalah is a tradition that uses a unique, symbolic language to interpret holy scripture. It has been frequently called *mysticism*, but that is a poor generalization. Kabbalah is a singular phenomenon and defies most attempts to strictly classify it. Among mystical and esoteric traditions where it's often included, it stands out for many reasons, but it is the *objective* of Kabbalah to integrate new ideas, without upsetting tradition, which I suggest, truly sets it apart. This integrative goal, I also suspect, has much to model for the benefit of freemasons and Freemasonry.

Kabbalah emerged from the Middle Ages as a product of competing ideas within Judaism. To give historical context, the Roman destruction of the Second Temple in the first century brought an end not only to the temple but to the temple priests who presided over the popular faith. Since then, the Jewish religion had been administered by rabbis who maintained the customs and rituals among the people. In the twelfth century, the influence of a new stream of philosophy, led by Rabbi Moses ben Maimon, better known as Maimonides (1138–1204), challenged many of the ancient Jewish concepts of God.

The traditional God of Judaism is very personal and closely involved with the people. He appears to them and answers their prayers. He guides them and dwells among them. He rejoices in their righteous acts and punishes their misdeeds. This God, so affected by, and involved with, the everyday activities of humans was in stark contrast to God as imagined by Maimonides who agreed largely with classical philosophers. Their *Primal Being*, by whatever name, was impersonal, immovable, inconceivable, the first cause, exalted and perfect, singular, undivided, and co-existent with no other.

Exposed to Greek and Arab philosophy, Maimonides introduced ideas that were previously foreign to Judaism. The philosophers' concepts of the perfection and purity of the Divine, increasingly conflicted with popular mythology. The God of the philosophers was eternal and infinite, lacking nothing and knowing everything. This invariably led to questions. Why would a perfect and self-sufficient deity need people to obey a book full of rules? What concern would an eternal and unchanging God have for the prayers or plight of humans?

The ideas presented in Maimonides's great work, *A guide for the perplexed*, with its rational God, had an appeal to intellectuals, but were otherwise very controversial. The distant and unapproachable deity of philosophy, could not provide the same comfort as the loving God of tradition. Though philosophy's influence was relatively limited, the hold which the rabbis struggled to retain on the religious heart of the Jewish people, was already strained by the encroachment of Christianity and Islam. Judaism was in no position to risk being further weakened by disunity within. Kabbalah, without directly confessing as much, sought to harmonize the seemingly irreconcilable ideas of the philosophers with the tradition of the rabbis. It delivers both the transcendent god, eternal and forever unchanged, and the personal God, present and participating in the world. Both are borne in a robust, dynamic, and amazingly creative description of a complex Godhead, encompassing every aspect of divinity. By providing a vehicle for contemporary ideas to coexist with established tradition, Kabbalah became important in preserving Judaism in the face of mounting threats to its existence.

Rabbi Moses ben Maimon, better known as Maimonides, or the Rambam, was a philosopher who challenged Jewish tradition.

Those who, today, task themselves with the stewardship of Masonry might find inspiration in those rabbis who preserved tradition amid the advance of contemporary thought. The minds and souls who gave the earliest voice to Kabbalah were not willing to sacrifice all the beauty and harmony of tradition. They imagined a way to preserve it. In many ways they were remarkably successful. Judaism not only survives but frequently does so as a picture of rich tradition co-existing with progressive thinking. This is a testament to Jewish spiritual leaders over the past two millennia and their creativity, of which some of the finest output produced the Kabbalah.

The ways in which Kabbalah can be helpful and relevant to Freemasonry are numerous. To begin with and above all else, Judaism is a monotheistic religion. There cannot be two different gods. The philosophers and rabbis being so far apart in their thinking seemed to mean one was right and the other simply had to be wrong. No explanation including multiple gods would be acceptable. The solution required one God that satisfied all descriptions. This was the great accomplishment of the kabbalists: combining the abstract god of the philosophers with the personal God of the rabbis. The complex deity they imagined answered all charges. *One God for everybody.* Most importantly, they found the answer they were looking for in the tradition they already had.

Kabbalah's answer to Judaism's medieval crisis provides possible help for Masonry today. First, it shows that tradition doesn't have to be changed to be modernized. This is a valuable example for Freemasonry as an institution. Kabbalists didn't change the Bible, just how it was interpreted, or rather how it *could be* interpreted. They gave people a way to see what they'd always seen, but see it in a new light. Legends and myths were readorned with symbolic meaning and new understandings were portrayed by old symbols. To be meaningful in contemporary culture, Masonry doesn't have to change its symbols. It can teach members how to interpret the symbols in a contemporary context and find meaning in them for themselves.

For masons attempting to reconcile their own philosophical or spiritual views with the symbols of Freemasonry, Kabbalah offers a novel approach. When dealing with mundane and finite objects as symbols of the sublime and the infinite, a certain amount of paradox is, perhaps, unavoidable. The creative solutions applied by kabbalists to the most difficult questions of faith and existence, provide a chart for sorting out the many conflicts of logic, sensation, and experience that make up human life. Our inheritance is the generous vocabulary of symbols which Kabbalah donates, along with a set of techniques for interpreting biblical scripture and symbolism in general.

Though people are surrounded by symbols, or maybe for that reason, most don't give much thought to them. Masonry and Kabbalah are both symbolic systems, and this is what makes them compatible. Masonry being, as mentioned, a system of morality, pertains to the mason's relationship with self and others. Kabbalah, on the other hand, is a religiophilosophical system and concerns the relationships with divinity and existence. Because a person's morality ultimately reflects their understanding of the truth, any morality is, in the end, difficult if not impossible to separate from religion. For this reason, a religious element is deeply enmeshed with the traditions of Freemasonry. At this intersection of morality and religion, Kabbalah and Masonry find their meeting point.

Central though they are, not just to Freemasonry and Kabbalah, but to all of human thought and communication, symbols are not often considered nor is symbolism often well understood. A brief introduction to symbolism, therefore, will be helpful.

Symbolism

What is a symbol and how do symbols work?

Symbolism, it may seem obvious, refers to the use of symbols to represent ideas. A symbol is, in the simplest description, one thing understood to stand for another thing. Letters and numbers are basic symbols. Words are symbols too. In a sense, all communication relies on symbols. The discussion of symbols started with ancient philosophers. In a modern, scholastic context, it now belongs to a field called *semiotics*, the study of signs.* While an in-depth treatment of semiotics is beyond both my ability and the intended scope of this book, some discussion of semiotics is required in any informed explanation of symbolism. Therefore a brief explanation of the terminology and jargon will be helpful to avoid misunderstanding.

In the jargon of semiotics, the term *sign* not only refers to what we normally think of as a sign—like a street sign or a business sign—but is a more general term, similar perhaps to how we commonly use the word *symbol*. The term *symbol*, in semiotic jargon, has a more narrow meaning and often refers only to a very specific type of sign. Technical jargon can be confusing to lay readers and in this case I believe it probably is. To avoid confusing readers, the word *symbol* is used throughout as most people understand it—something representing something else. Trying not to misrepresent the work of semioticians, their preferred word, *sign*, will also be used in the same general sense. Except where specifically indicated, the two words are used practically interchangeably.

In the nineteenth century, Swiss linguist Ferdinand de Saussure was among the first to attempt to define a modern study of systems of signs.† According to Saussure, a sign consists of two parts—the signifier and the signified. The signifier, is what you see.‡ It's the representation. The signified is the idea or object that is being represented. For example, the word "boat," whether written or spoken, signifies an actual boat. The word is the signifier and the actual boat (or at least your understanding of what an actual boat is), is the signified. For something to be a sign, Saussure points out, both parts are necessary. A signifier must have

---

* Not symbology. Apologies to many Dan Brown fans.

† Saussure avoided using the term *symbol* in his general discourse on signs, reserving that term for a special type of sign, what are referred to here as *conventional* symbols.

‡ Or hear or smell or envision; it's what is presented to your senses or imagination.

something that it signifies. A thing only becomes a symbol when it stands for something else.

Around that same time, American philosopher Charles S. Peirce (pronounced *purse*), independently developed his own sign theory. He described signs as having three parts. The sign doesn't just stand for the object. It has to be, Peirce says, interpreted by somebody to stand for the object. He added a third part, the interpretant, which is the individual's translation or interpretation of the sign. Without this part, says Peirce, nothing is a sign. A thing only becomes a symbol when *someone understands it* to stand for something else.

A symbol doesn't have meaning by itself. It acquires meaning only when a person attaches meaning to it. The way in which symbols acquire meaning is not the same for all symbols. Some are arbitrarily chosen to represent something else. The letters of the alphabet are a perfect example of this. Each letter is arbitrarily assigned to a phonetic sound which it represents. There is no reason a particular letter should represent any certain sound, except that it has been assigned to do so by popular convention. Nothing about the written character itself tells us anything about the sound it symbolizes. We simply agree that a letter represents a certain sound and so it does. Symbols like these are called *conventional* symbols because they rely on a cultural or social convention.

Other types of symbols don't rely on convention but acquire meaning by their similarity to something else. Sometimes called *iconic* symbols, there is a sameness between themselves and the object they represent.[§] A triangle, for example, because it has three sides, may become a symbol for anything that has three parts. An equilateral triangle, by the equal measure of its angles, could be a symbol of equality. A triangle might symbolize one thing because it appears to point upward and another thing when it points down. In these cases, the triangle resembles the objects or concepts it symbolizes, either by its physical appearance (having

---

§ There are other types of signs, e.g., natural signs, such as smoke being a sign of fire, which are classified by Peirce as 'indexical.' General types are provided here as a conceptual aid. As will be seen, classifying signs is not clean work. Not all semioticians agree on the types, and signs can, and often do, simultaneously possess characteristics of more than one type.

three sides, appearing to point in a particular direction) or an abstract quality it possesses (equality).

Different people might interpret the same symbol differently, even when they agree about what it symbolizes. Take for example, two people who both believe that an eagle represents freedom. One of them, as a child, was told this by his father. Throughout his life, each time he saw an eagle, he

The triangle, representing the three-part waste reduction initiative Reduce, Reuse, Recycle, is a symbol for recyclable material.

remembered what it stands for and he thought of freedom. The other person was never told any such thing. She thinks of the nearly limitless heights to which the eagle can soar and to her this unbounded flight resembles freedom. In the end, they both see the same symbol, an eagle, and recall the same concept, freedom, but it would be wrong to say that they both saw the same meaning in the symbol. The interpretation gives the symbol its meaning.

Contemplating by symbols

Symbols are not only how we communicate but how we think and understand. Conventional symbols such as letters, numbers, and traffic signals are used every day in all areas of our lives, and we interpret them so automatically that most of us don't even think of them as symbols representing something. The relationship is so close that the object— that is, the thing symbolized—can seem to be a property of the symbol. What I mean by this is, if you ask about the relationship between a letter and a sound, a common response would be to say that a letter *makes* a sound. Few would say that the letter *represents* the sound. We say that a word *means* such and such, not that it *represents* such and such concept.

For some systems to be effective—letters, numbers, and words, for example—the interpretation cannot deviate from convention. A person can't be free to reinterpret the symbol for themself. Imagine each person assigning different sounds to the letters of the alphabet. Reading and writing would be impossible. Conventional symbols are extremely useful for formal communication exactly because they are far less open to interpretation. Traffic lights wouldn't work if it was left up to each driver to decide what red means to them.

The other types of symbols, those that don't rely on convention, share a resemblance or indexical relationship with their object. They possess some quality that describes or represents the object. Something you know about the symbol is also, in some way, apparently true about the object it symbolizes. A scale, because it portrays balance, is often a symbol of justice. Balance suggests an idea of equality, and equality is important to our concept of justice. Equality isn't the same as justice, but it is an aspect of it. Equality is each getting the same, justice is each getting what they deserve. However, it will be impossible to give everybody what they deserve, if people do not enjoy equal opportunities and equal protection. The equality we see in the scale represents that same part of justice.

In addition to equality, a scale might represent other ideas that would further suggest justice. For example, the idea of weighing something suggests a trial. We put something on a scale to try it, to see if it is what it should be, whether it is more or less than we expect or want to permit. Justice also requires a trial to "weigh" the evidence and ascertain the facts. Additionally, justice demands a fair correspondence between actions and consequences. Reward or punishment should never be too great or too small but should, in every case, match the deed.

All of these ideas—equal protection under the law, a trial of the facts, and actions having appropriate consequences—are simultaneously suggested by the symbol of the scale. Each new interpretation seems to enrich the idea of the scale as a symbol of justice. Symbols in this way often surpass words in their abilities to communicate concepts, especially those that consist of more complex and nuanced ideas like justice or, as in the previous example, freedom.

Imagine the impossible

Because interpretation of symbols occurs in the interpreter's mind, neither the symbol nor the object symbolized has to be real. In the example above, the eagle represents the intangible idea of freedom. We can't see or touch freedom but we can define it. Peirce suggested anything can be discussed if it can be defined, even if the definition doesn't make sense. He points out that things can be defined that can't actually exist. In his example, he imagines a hypothetical object, an *OG*, which he defines as "a four-sided triangle." Even though it's impossible to have the concept of a four-sided triangle, a conversation about its impossibility can be had. A four-sided triangle can't exist or even be conceived, but it can still be the topic of discussion

There is a reason a four-sided triangle can't be conceived. It is an impossibility—a contradiction that can't be true in any way we can imagine. One concept, a shape with three sides, is simply incompatible with the other concept of four-sidedness. Trying to imagine a shape that simultaneously is three-sided and four-sided is not possible. However, not everything that can't be conceived is impossible. Some things simply exceed our ability to fully imagine because they are limitless. Infinity is one such example.

Justice depicted holding a scale.

Infinity is defined as having no limits in size or extent.* This is completely unintuitive to human experience. Nothing is infinite. Even the universe itself (if we are to believe current estimates) is, at ninety-three billion light years across, unimaginably enormous but not infinite.†

---

* unlimited extent of time, space, or quantity : boundlessness https://www.merriam-webster.com/dictionary/infinity

† Even an expanding universe, though growing, is at any point in time, finite.

Despite straining the imagination to conceive of size to the greatest extent possible, no one can ever truly conceive *infinite* size. If this is frustrating, it's nonetheless how the brain has to work. Evolutionarily speaking, it's much more important for organisms to be able to tell where one thing ends and where something else begins than to contemplate unending space. So our brains evolved to understand the world in finite concepts—we recognize this thing is different from that thing.

Although humans have, for who knows how long now, enjoyed speculating about the unlimited, we do so using limited concepts. The unlimited—infinity, eternity—becomes limited; limited to a single discreet concept. The act of defining something makes it finite. A definition *is* a limit. It establishes a thing as itself, only itself, and no other thing. Any one thing must end where another begins. Defining a concept sets the boundary between that idea and all other ideas. Humans can't perfectly picture infinity, but we can talk about it because we can define it. Using the definition above, we'll follow the example of an infinity of size.[‡]

To imagine something infinitely large, we take the separate concepts used in the definition—size and limitlessness—and consider them individually. Thinking, for example, of the vastness of the universe, extending to the very bounds of imagination, gives an idea of immense, but still not limitless, size. Separately, one can envision an endless course, traced without limit around a figure-eight, and have a concept of limitlessness without any regard for size. We can't imagine limitless size, but we can imagine limitlessness on one hand and size on the other, and aggregate an idea from those pieces. This is how we contemplate the inconceivable: by way of the conceivable qualities we use to define it.

Infinity, again, is not intuitive. We live in a finite world and our language describes finite things. Our imperfect conception of infinity comes from the simple fact that the concepts we are trying to separate just don't come apart cleanly. We usually refer to space in terms of size or quantity. *How much space?* Our definition, unlimited space, attempts to remove the concept of limits from the concept of space and therefore

---

[‡] As opposed to an infinity of value which would have served just as well for an example.

from the consideration of size. However, size is a measurement and a thing without limits can't be measured. Removing the concept of *limits* thoroughly and unavoidably confuses the concept of *size*. To speak of a thing's "infinite size" is effectively to speak of its "immeasurable measurement."

Despite the fact that these concepts don't fit together perfectly, "infinite space" is not a logical paradox like a four-sided triangle. Infinity isn't impossible, it's just impossible for us to imagine perfectly. While it was correct to say "nothing is infinite," it is not equally correct to say, "there is no infinity." Mathematics makes great use of infinity and, in many applications, treats it as a real number. It is both our blessing and our curse as humans that we can talk about, think about, and even rely upon, things that we really can't even imagine—at least not fully; not intuitively. We use the things we know as symbols of the things we can't know but can only talk and think about.

This is how humans experience and interpret the world: by way of symbols. Whether a person realizes it or not, everything they see, at least everything they recognize or understand, is a symbol. In fact, things often symbolizes more than one idea at the same time. For example, when you see a shih tzu in the park, your mind simultaneously recalls the concept you have of a *dog*, along with the separate one you may have of a *little dog*, and perhaps, if you are familiar with the very loveable breed, the specific concept of a *shih tzu*.

Different symbols can symbolize the same thing too. If instead of *seeing* a dog, imagine you heard a dog bark. The same concept of a dog would come to your mind. An auditory signal, the sound of the bark, replaces the visual one, but your mind still arrives at the same idea of a dog. The thing you sense is separate and distinct from the concept it brings to mind. Just as a word might have more than one meaning and an object has a different name in every language, so every concept is separated from the words, names, pictures, sounds, smells, tastes, or feelings that symbolize it.

Two people who agree that a symbol represents a specific concept, don't have to share the same ideas. In fact, they very well may not. They may, as in the earlier example of the eagle, see the same thing in a symbol but have completely different reasons for seeing it. The two agreed that an eagle is a symbol of freedom, but if asked why, would have given significantly different answers. They may further disagree about the definition of the concept being represented, freedom. Returning to the example of the shih tzu in the park, everybody has a concept of a dog. While most of us probably have some details in common, everybody has their own, different, concept of a dog. Is a dog a beloved pet or a smelly animal? It depends who you ask. Are little dogs cute or annoying? It depends who you ask. Is a shih tzu loveable? That one, of course, is a trick question. Yes, they are.

Communicating with symbols

From the beginning of civilization and likely before, people have employed the great capacity of symbols to convey layers of meaning richly and often beautifully. Masonry and Kabbalah each make extensive use of symbols, both conventional and iconic. Freemasonry, attempting to address concerns over membership numbers, has in many places simplified its system. This, unfortunately, provided little of the intended effect and the efforts have, by some, been regarded negatively. A feature of masonic education that specifically suffered—to the point of nearly being lost—is the practice of interpreting symbols. As a result, the symbols eventually all become matters of convention.

While all symbols share some characteristics in common, conventional and iconic symbols are different in very important practical ways. Conventional symbols are relied upon for clarity in communication and identification. The meaning of these symbols must be agreed upon by all for them to be effective. So the group decides their meaning. They aren't up to individual interpretation. You don't get to decide that the big red octagon posted at the corner means something different to you. It means "stop." On the other hand, iconic symbols are, as they say, in the eye of the beholder. The interpretation of these types of symbols belongs entirely to the observer.* If something represents an idea to you, nobody can suggest it doesn't. Iconic symbols recall something in the mind of the individual.

Symbols can be, and often are, both iconic and conventional. Sometimes they are both at once. Like when numbers acquire spiritual significance. Other times they start as iconic but become conventional. Computer icons might be an example of this. In the early days of graphic computers, icons were chosen because they were believed to be intuitive. Users, it was hoped, would interpret the meaning without having to be told. However, with certain functions, e.g., *save* and *print*, being common to many applications, many of the symbols became standardized.

Though the world has changed a lot since the 1980s, computer icons, relatively speaking, have not. Many of the objects still depicted in computer icons are no longer used in real life and some aren't even recognizable by younger generations. Representations of floppy disks and telephone receivers are both still widely seen icons in 2025, however neither of those objects is easily found in the "real world" anymore. There are other "symbols" in the language of computing—carbon copies, address books, radio buttons—that at one time referred to common objects but are now understood only as matters of convention. It's likely that anyone born in the twenty-first century has only ever seen or "used" any of those things on the screen of a computer or mobile device.

Graphic icons (clockwise from top-left) Save, Phone, Movie, and Voicemail, are still common despite the fact that floppy disks, telephone handsets, film reels, and audio tapes are not.

Once upon a time, computer icons were easily interpreted symbols; now they are learned arbitrarily. The reason they signify

---

* Although the observer will invariably decode it according to some language which will influence its meaning.

anything at all is increasingly likely to be explained as "it just does." This is what has become of a great number of Masonry's symbols. Many masons can identify the symbols by name and most of them can tell you what they conventionally represent, but few anymore can tell you *why* a particular symbol might have a particular meaning.

Fourteenth century painting. A woman teaches geometry to ten pupils. In her left hand she holds a square, with her right she uses a compass.

CHAPTER 2

The Symbols

Symbols of Masonry

The symbols of Freemasonry are almost entirely acquired from other sources. The material symbols primarily derive from the physical tools of stonemasons and builders, but owe also to astrology, alchemy, classical mythology, Greek philosophy, and Judeo-Christian religious iconography. To modern eyes they may look like a collection of antiquarian oddities, sundry and mismatched tokens of a past that is near enough to be vaguely familiar but too distant to be relatable. However, a closer look at these symbols suggests something interesting about the intent and efforts of Masonry's modern founders.

Alchemy and astrology, despite their modern disrepute, were the natural sciences of seventeenth century Europe. Many of the brilliant minds of the Royal Society, including its long-serving president, Isaac Newton (1643–1727), occupied themselves with exactly these pursuits. However, science (or "natural philosophy" as it was then commonly called) seemed to many at the time dangerously close to magic. Progressive, humanist thinking as well often sounded, to the prejudiced or unsophisticated ear, like disagreement with the church. Both of these were the most serious heresy, and in the 1600s heresy was not easily tolerated. Newton became famous for proving many of the same ideas for which Giordano Bruno (1548–1600) had been burned to death just a few generations earlier.

Though public belief in magical ideas was slowly waning by the beginning of the eighteenth century, religious and royal authorities were not yet liberal on the matter. In 1717, when Masonry's first grand lodge was taking its beginning, England and Scotland were less than a year removed from the executions of Mary and Elizabeth Hicks, hanged as witches in Huntingdon and said to be the last such case in England.[16] It would still be another five years or so before an elderly and mentally unfit woman in the town of Dornoch would be the last in Scotland. Still plaguing much of Europe, was brutal religious intolerance, exemplified strikingly by the French persecution of the Huguenots and the Spanish Inquisition. The Europe that gave birth to Masonry was and would remain religiously violent and dangerous. More than a hundred years after the Grand Lodge's first assembly, the Inquisition would finally claim its last official victim, a deist schoolteacher, in 1826.

The men who wrote the "New Constitutions" of Masonry were well aware that, although significant progress was being made, the enlightened future they foresaw, had not yet arrived. J.T. Desaguliers, perhaps the chief architect of the new grand lodge, had himself arrived in England as the young child of fleeing Huguenot parents. Desaguliers and his fellows, wisely chose to establish the new institution in as strong and safe a position as possible. There could be nothing about the group that might be considered heretical or opposed to royal authority or national traditions. Aware of the real danger of religious persecution, they maintained a Christian, albeit non-denominational, appearance. Understanding the importance of tradition in European society, they linked themselves to the "ancient" lodges.

Mentioned earlier, a particular requirement of medieval lodges, belief in a Trinitarian god, was modified to a belief in a "religion upon which all Men agree." This allowed for diverse membership but also protected the group from any identity that might be viewed unfavorably. Every lodge was, at least nominally, Christian and was visibly furnished with a Bible. Additionally, the ritual and attendant legends contained numerous references to biblical characters. By twenty-first century Western standards, such overt Christianity might be interpreted as intolerant of diverse faith or spirituality, and itself be controversial. However, in Britain in 1723, it was an absolutely nonnegotiable requirement of the group's existence.

Since masons held their meetings privately and kept their dealings secret, they were naturally the target of suspicion. With civil war and revolution a constant fear, secret societies filled both religious and royal authorities with misgivings. For this reason, it was also important that Masonry require members to very openly declare their patriotism and loyalty to their country. Medieval stonemasons, builders of magnificent cathedrals and splendid castles throughout Europe, pledged their allegiance and service to the king. The New Charges, reflecting modern developments, would require freemasons to be loyal to the "supreme legislature" and to "never be concerned" in plots against the government.

By connecting itself to the ancient lodges, even fancifully, Freemasonry inherited in appearance and reputation the profile of a long-standing partner with royal and civic authorities, dutiful in service to God and religion. This conservative framework, which carefully preserved the appearance of the Old Charges, was decorated with modern ideas of philosophy, science, history, and religion. Along with the inclusion of natural science, were elements of Greek philosophy and ancient myth. While neither of these was, itself, modern, the appreciation and understanding of them was. Lost for centuries in Europe and finally made available by Marsilio Ficino's fifteenth century Latin translation, the works of Plato, Aristotle, and others were greeted by many as a restoration of ancient wisdom. The same is true of the Greco-Egyptian Hermetic writings, for the first modern translation of which we may also thank Ficino.

> the Lodge confifted of a young Prince of an illu-
> ftrious Houfe, two other Princes, fix Counts of
> the greateft Houfes in Auftria, four Generals, a
> Foreign Minifter well known among the *Literati*,
> and three Ecclefiafticks in Priefts Orders : In this
> Number there are Roman Catholicks, Proteftants
> and Lutherans ; for the Free Mafons admit Per-
> fons of all Religions, even Mahometans, nay, fuch
> as have no Religion at all. But what moft furpri-

A 1743 Edinburgh newspaper reports the raid of a Viennese masonic lodge by Austrian authorities. Lodge membership was religiously diverse and included royalty, military officers, state officials, scholars and, surprisingly, clergy.

The largest portion of Masonry's symbols and ritual, including all that was legitimately inherited from craft guilds and anything pretended to be ancient, was Christian in nature. This remains true today. While in the past overt religious signaling had the effect of normalizing Freemasonry's outward appearance, today in many places it has the opposite effect. Because of this, the group is often unfairly categorized by both religious and secular critics who misunderstand Masonry's use of those symbols. Masonry's place in future society may very well hinge on how it answers that criticism.

Symbols of Kabbalah

Kabbalah, unlike Masonry, does not maintain any material symbols. Instead it has for its symbols a homegrown vocabulary of words. No discussion of Kabbalah is possible (at least no meaningful discussion) without some reference to its defining symbols, known as the *sephirot*. However, since these symbols are unique to Kabbalah, most will find some introduction helpful. To begin with, the word *sephirot* (pronounced with a long ō, like boat) is plural and only exists in the vocabulary of Kabbalah. In total, there are ten *sephirot*. The singular form is *sephirah* and the etymology of the word is mysterious.

The *sephirot*, as was said, belong entirely to the vocabulary of Kabbalah and exist nowhere outside of that context. The word first appears in a very old text called the *Sefer Yetzirah*. There, ten "*sephirot of nothingness*" are mentioned as being among the materials God used to form the world. Early kabbalistic texts from the end of the twelfth century began to reference those mysterious *sephirot*, gradually expanding the term to include an increasing number of different ideas. They were, in different works by different kabbalists, described as spheres, identified as divine attributes, and related to the creative sayings ("*Let there be light*," etc.) uttered by God in the biblical book of Genesis.

Through the end of the thirteenth century, the symbolism attached to the *sephirot* expanded in fantastic, creative ways. Generally speaking

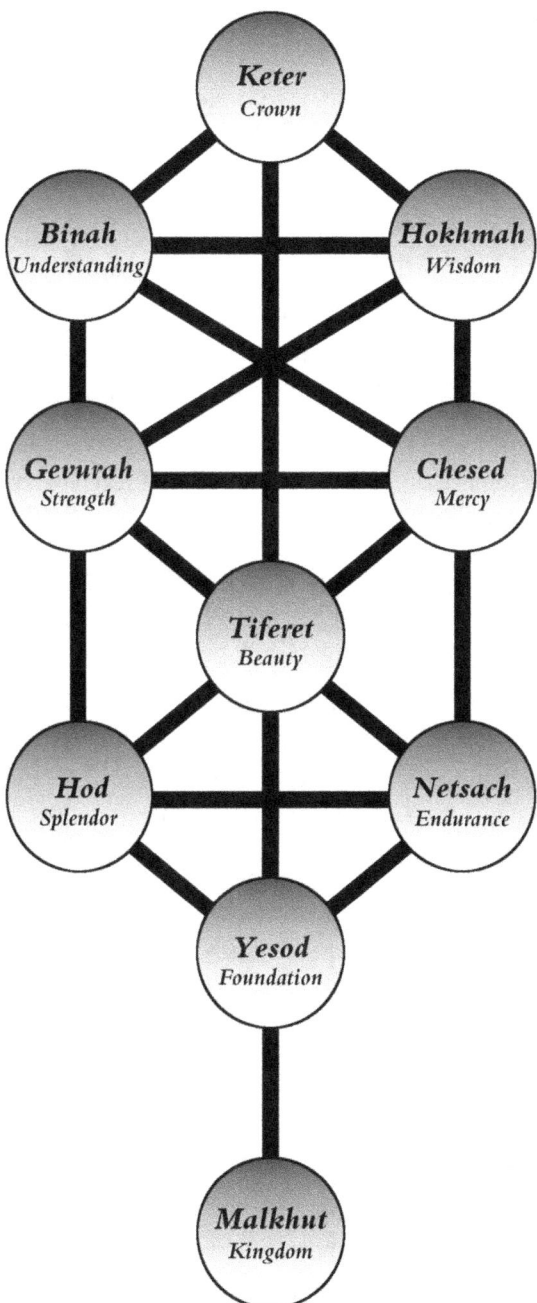

Etz Chaim, the *Tree of Life*, displaying the *sephirot*. These are the key symbols of Kabbalah.

the crowning achievement of this great output is a voluminous collection of texts known as the *Zohar*, which first appeared in Spain in the last decade of the thirteenth century. In it, nearly the entire Hebrew Bible is cast into the symbols of the *sephirot*. Every story is retold as another carefully encoded account in the ongoing saga of Creation, which, in Kabbalah, is really the *only* story.

The *sephirot* are often explained as divine emanations or attributes. Neither explanation is perfect, but both are useful in specific contexts. The *sephirot* emerge in succession from the unknowable heights of the Godhead. The first is called *Keter*, a Hebrew word for *Crown*. The others proceed in order, each emanating from the previous one and inheriting the undiminished essence of divinity. Each one receives a portion of *all* of the divine attributes in a mixture befitting its position and individual nature. The result is that one attribute is emphasized and comes to define each *sephirah*. The final sephirah is called *Malkhut*, the *Kingdom*, and symbolizes, among other things, God's presence in the world.

Each of the *sephirot* has a proper name, usually, but not necessarily reflecting its defining attribute. Listed in order by their Hebrew names (English translation in parentheses), they proceed as follows:

Keter (Crown), *Hokhmah* (Wisdom), *Binah* (Understanding), *Chesed* (Mercy), *Gevurah* (Strength), *Tif'eret* (Beauty), *Netzach* (Endurance), *Hod* (Glory), *Yesod* (Foundation), and *Malkhut* (Kingdom).

Several sephirot are alternately referred to by other names. *Keter* is known as *Ratzon* (Will), *Chesed* is sometimes called *Gedulah* (Greatness) and *Gevurah* also has the name *Din* (Judgment). In addition to these, all of them have a number of symbolic nicknames, cognomina, and aliases, many of which will be introduced throughout this book.

The *sephirot* are occasionally described as a series of concentric circles or spheres. This symbolism is not widely employed, but is at times helpful to illustrate some peculiar aspects of their subtle nature. This arrangement is only rarely referred to. Far more common is the placement of the ten sephirot in the familiar pattern known by the Hebrew name, *Etz Chaim*, the Tree of Life.

The Tree of Life (see previous) arranges the *sephirot*, first in three columns: right, left, and center. The right and left columns, or pillars as they're often called, represent two sides balanced by a center column. Some readers will know them as representing *Mercy* and *Judgment*. This is a very popular interpretation but of course there are others. The *pillars* might represent any set of complementary concepts. Not necessarily opposites, they stand for any two qualities which can be introduced to each other for the mutual benefit of both; male and female or wisdom and strength, for example.

The Tree of Life, also arranged in vertical levels, additionally introduces a hierarchy to the *sephirot*. Interpretations vary concerning the number of levels, but two images recur frequently. In one, the *sephirot* are imagined with the first nine, grouped into three descending groups of three. This hierarchy vaguely resembles that of classical Greek and later Neoplatonist ideas regarding *levels* of existence. The highest triad, *Keter-Hokhmah-Binah*, correspond to the divine mind, an abstract or intellectual realm. The second threesome, *Chesed-Gevurah-Tif'eret* form a divine heart, symbolizing an emotional level. The lower three, *Netzach-Hod-Yesod* are the divine foundation, a level of sensation. The *sephirot* culminate in *Malkhut*, who is unique. She is the divine presence in the world, reflecting divine light to the physical world.

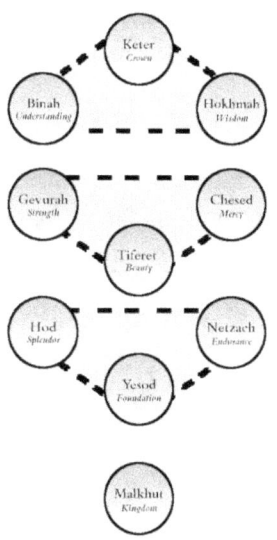

The three triads of the sephirot with Malkhut below.

Commonly, the triad of *Keter-Hokhmah-Binah* are said to be *hidden* and apart from the lower seven. These, the first sephirot to emerge, do not present themselves to the world below.

The lower seven are the *revealed* aspects of divinity. They represent attributes of God that people can comprehend and experience. The seven may be broken down further, but one sephirah, *Malkhut*, as was said, is unique. Kabbalistic tradition often portrays the six from *Chesed* to *Yesod*, coming together and being harmonized or balanced in *Tif'eret*, the sixth sephirah. Because the six of them are balanced by the *sixth* one of them, the group is collectively symbolized by the sixth Hebrew letter, ו (*vav*), which is also the number six. References to *Tif'eret*, especially using the nickname *heaven* or *the heavens*, are at times, by proxy, to the six of them.

The critical distinction between *Malkhut* and the other six is, while the rest are inseparable from each other, *Malkhut* can be disconnected from the group. The others are more thoroughly interconnected but *Malkhut* depends upon a tenuous connection, which at times can be broken. This unusual vulnerability is part of a major theme of Kabbalah; *Malkhut*, the last sephirah, represents the *Shekinah*, that aspect of God that traditionally dwells among the people. The presence of God among the people, that is, the idea of *Divine Providence*, central to Kabbalah, is also an important symbol in Freemasonry. In the most practical way, it represents the interconnectedness of humans to the world we live in.

In Kabbalah, the good deeds of righteous people below, stimulate blessings from above. A primary occupation of the *sephirot* is providing for this transfer in both directions. When humans stop performing acts of charity, the divine effluence is diminished. When the people behave badly enough, the paths that connect the *sephirot* become damaged, further inhibiting the flow. Subjected to enough neglect, the blessings of Heaven may cease to reach the world below. The biblical story of the exile in Babylon, is, according to Kabbalah, a symbolic example of the divine network suffering neglect. When blessing is withheld from the people, *Malkhut* is also cut off. Deriving from the Hebrew word for *dwelling*, the *Shekinah* is intimately connected with the people. The divine presence never departs from them, even if that means following them into *exile*. In this way, *Malkhut* is uniquely susceptible to influences of the material world, which include the forces of evil.

Malkhut is further distinguished by being the last of the *sephirot*. The outflow of divinity is received by each *sephirah* from the one preceding it and given to the one following it. However *Malkhut* is last, emanating no more beyond itself, and so only receives. The world below *Malkhut*, which is not divine, can never receive the divinity from above. Instead, divinity is reflected by *Malkhut* for the material world to see, like the moon reflecting the light of the sun. Symbolically, such receptive power is considered *female*. Accordingly, the *Shekinah* is known as a divine feminine or one of the female expressions of God. As the divine presence, the part of God accessible in the world, *Malkhut* is center stage in many of the stories of Kabbalah.

The Zohar, Sefer Yetzirah, and the writings of Kabbalah

Though there is no universally accepted canon for Kabbalah, the volumes that make up the work known as the *Zohar*, would certainly have to be included in any sensible list. Those familiar with Kabbalah have certainly heard of the *Zohar*. Few, however, are likely to have read more than a small portion of this tremendous and voluminous text. It is, without debate, the central text of Kabbalah and undoubtedly its most important work. Throughout the chapters that follow, you will be presented with the abstruse wisdom of this masterpiece of spiritual symbolism. Written in thirteenth century Spain, it no doubt contains wisdom passed forward from the unknown recesses of the remote past.

Be warned. The secrets of the *Zohar* must be earned. Whatever wisdom is gleaned from its pages will not be without effort. The *Zohar* is formidable. First, it is massive. A modern critical English translation, the exquisite Pritzker Edition, is available in twelve large volumes. Other English translations reflecting varying scholarship, and with considerably fewer explanatory notes, exist in as few as five volumes. The majority of the *Zohar* texts were written in a stylized Aramaic. Full of neologisms and loan words from Latin, Arabic, and Spanish, it is famously hard to read and has challenged patient and erudite scholars. Finally, it was written in an intentionally mysterious, multi-layered symbolism that obscures the true meaning from those uninitiated into the unique language of Kabbalah, the language of the *sephirot*.

Aside from the *Zohar* (and the ubiquitous *Sefer Yetzirah* which belongs to a class with nothing else), the literature of Kabbalah can be thought of in two categories. First, are writings which followed the *Zohar* and reconciled a great deal of its many strangenesses. This includes primarily the works of Moshe Cordevero, who organized the wild mass of Kabbalah in his extensive and most important work *Pardes Rimonim*, and most famously Isaac Luria. The latter was known as "the Arizal," often shortened to "the Ari," Hebrew for *lion*. The Ari is largely considered to be the final important contributor to Kabbalah and his opinions still carry, for many, the utmost authority. It may, therefore, be surprising that he left no writings of his own. His teachings are only known through the publications of his students, particularly Chaim Vital, and later exponents, like Joseph Ergas whose *Shomer Emunim* is as clear a presentation of Luria's ideas, and Kabbalah in general, as could be hoped for.

The second group of kabbalistic texts are those which preceded or were contemporary with the *Zohar*. Of these "early works," the anonymous book *Bahir*, the writings of Isaac the Blind and others of the so-called *Illyun* circle in Provence, France, and Joseph Gikatilla's *Gates of Light*, which came from the same Castilian milieu that produced the *Zohar*, can't be overlooked. These writings sowed the seeds of many concepts later brought fully to life in the *Zohar*. The works I've named here do not, by any means, represent all the important writings of Kabbalah. There are many more that are not included. Some are relatively well known and some are absolutely obscure, but each has in some time and in some way contributed to Kabbalah. However, for the scope of this book, the works mentioned here and selected as examples later are enough to present a full and well-rounded overview of Kabbalah, particularly where it relates to Freemasonry.

THE
CONSTITUTIONS
OF THE
FREE-MASONS.

CONTAINING THE

History, Charges, Regulations, &c.
of that moſt Ancient and Right
Worſhipful *FRATERNITY.*

For the Uſe of the LODGES.

LONDON:
Printed by WILLIAM HUNTER, for JOHN SENEX at the *Globe,*
and JOHN HOOKE at the *Flower-de-luce* over-againſt St. Dunſtan's
Church, in Fleet-ſtreet.

In the Year of Maſonry ———— 5723
Anno Domini ———— 1723

Title page of the 1723 Constitutions.

CHAPTER 3

A Religion Upon Which All Agree

Religion and Nature

Freemasonry's "religion upon which all Men agree" specifically obliged its members to follow the "Moral law" and to be "good men and true" regardless of their religious affiliation. The influences of natural philosophy and the science of the time, can be seen in the ideas that underlie the rules and regulations of the new Grand Lodge. The 1723 Constitutions, as the rules were called, carefully made room for progressive thought. In other writings of the time these influences, more than just suggested, were made explicitly clear. The curious book *Long Livers*, written in 1716 and translated into English in 1722, bears the following dedication:

> Most humbly dedicated to the Grand Master, Masters, Wardens and Brethren of the most Ancient and most Honourable Fraternity of the FREE-MASONS of *Great Britain* and *Ireland*

The author, a freemason himself, addressed a fifty-page opening directly to his fellows, in which is written the following:

> ... the Religion we profess, which is the best that ever was, or is, or can be; and whoever lives up to it can never perish eternally, for it is the Law of Nature, which is the Law of God, for God is Nature.

The influence of science within Freemasonry was apparently not limited to Desaguliers and the others who drafted the New Constitutions. The effort and expense required to translate and publish *Long Livers* in

English would reasonably suggest the book enjoyed some popularity. Nonetheless, this description of God as Nature is strikingly close to the one that had, only four generations earlier, resulted in the disrepute and banishment of Dutch philosopher Baruch de Spinoza (1632–1677). Excommunicated from the Jewish community at twenty-three years of age and his writings eventually outlawed by the Catholic church, the young Spinoza did not propose that there was no God—in fact, he insisted there was. His transgression was in dismantling traditional ideas. He claimed that God was not separate from but synonymous with nature. To both Jews and Christians, making the Creator equal to nature, which it created, was heresy. The founders of Freemasonry were not eager to commit such a mistake and deftly suggested, without recklessly overstating, any scientific or philosophical inclinations.

The bold and open-faced assertions made in such books as *Long Livers* were done anonymously under pen names. Dissimilarly, the authors of the New Constitutions, whatever their interest in progress, were not writing anonymously. They openly represented themselves and all freemasons and could not afford to be overly provocative. Though unquestionably influenced by natural science (Desaguliers was a Fellow of the Royal Society and close friend and assistant of Newton's), they prudently accepted tradition as a boundary to observe. The writers, primarily Desaguliers along with Rev. James Anderson and George Payne, cleverly worked to weave their new ideas as unobtrusively as possible into the old fabric. The result of that creativity remains, even today, the center of masonic belief, that religion upon which all agree.

Certainly, when the New Charges were written, the very idea of a religion upon which all might agree was quite different than it must be today. Along with a variety of traditional religions, there are also now many new spiritual denominations and philosophical schools. However, despite the wide range of opinions about the mysteries of the cosmos and life, there are certain points about which everybody must agree.* To

---

* There is an objective point where misaligned beliefs can only be attributed to dysregulated thought.

begin with, all of us regardless of our individual beliefs exist on the same planet, in the same world, defined by the same laws. Whether these are the *Law of God* or the *laws of nature* is, perhaps, only a semantic debate. These laws, by any name, preexisted the universe and determined its formation. Through all of time they remain unchanged and undiminished despite the universe itself constantly changing. Ascribed to God, nature, or anything else, they are the same laws, and all agree it's these which govern the universe.

These laws produce the world we live in, a world of cause and effect. Philosophers long ago arrived at the seemingly logical conclusion there must have been a *first cause*. Thousands of years later, one of the most compelling questions ever asked—*What is the first cause?*—is still not answered or answerable. Science now supposes, as many traditions long have, the universe that we know has not been here forever but has a definite, although still mysterious, beginning.

This is the starting point. Three things on which all can (or should be able to) agree. First, the universe exists; second, it has a beginning prior to which there was nothing; and third, the same universe is governed by a definite set of rules or laws. These are the principal tenets of a religion upon which all agree.

The Great Architect of the Universe

Early civilizations may not have understood as well as we do now, how the laws of nature worked, but everywhere they recognized that those rules produced an order to nature. Unimaginably complex and powerful beyond comparison, the world is conducted with a precision far exceeding that of any human system. Such orderly arrangement, it was imagined, could only be by the design of a Supreme Intelligence. Accordingly, the creation myths of many of the earliest known civilizations depict a Creator who calls the world to order out of chaos.

Some early traditions, interestingly, do not include a creation myth. These instead imagined the world having no beginning; it always was and always will be. The late professor Huston Smith describes why the concept of a Creator god executing a plan according to divine will, was an important development:

> For [the religions of] India, human destiny lies outside history altogether . . . Good and evil, pleasure and pain, right and wrong are woven into [the world] in relatively equal proportions . . . And so things will remain. All thought of cleaning up the world and changing its character appreciably is mistaken in principle. The nature religions . . . reached the same conclusion by a different route. For them human destiny lay within history . . . as currently constituted, not as it might become. We can see why change—specifically change for the better—did not suggest itself to nature religionists. If one's eye is on nature preeminently, one does not look beyond it for fulfillment elsewhere. But neither—and this is the point—does one dream of improving nature or the social order that is its extension, for these are assumed to be ingrained in the nature of things and not subject to human alteration . . . for in nature the accent is on what is, not what should be—the is rather than the ought. (Smith p. 284)

The god of the monotheistic ancient Hebrew tribes was different. Their God—who was the only god—created the world for a reason and according to a plan. This difference provided them with, among other things, a unique opportunity for *hopefulness*. Smith continues:

> Because nature was created by God, God could not be assimilated to it. The consequence of keeping God and nature distinct is momentous, for it means that the "ought" cannot be assimilated to the "is"— God's will transcends (and can differ from) immanent actuality. (Smith p. 285)

To affect positive change, one has to believe that *what is* does not necessarily reflect *what ought to be*. Acknowledging imperfections is the foundation for progress, both personally and socially. The search for something better, the drive to improve, both ourselves and the world around us, begins with the belief that our current state is not already perfect.

Today, a number of members echo the general public in asking why Masonry still maintains any connection to religion or spirituality at all. This question is not new. French lodges, long ago, did away with the faith requirement.* However regular Masonry maintains a connection to spirituality. Neither ignorant nor stubborn, Masonry is a system of morality. Morality, it's true, is different from religion, but the two are not entirely independent. Morality is the practice of ethics, which concerns itself with the questions of right and wrong behavior. To act morally, one must have an idea of right and wrong. What a person believes to be true directly impacts what we believe to be right and wrong, which influences our behavior in every area of life. Correct and incorrect belong to science. Right and wrong do not. To improve as an individual or as a member of their family and community, a freemason or any person must be willing to eliminate wrong behavior and replace it with what they believe is right.

To bring one's self, the community, or society as a whole closer to the state in which it *ought* to be, there requires an idea of what ought to be. The Great Architect of the Universe is more than a simple stand-in for any person's god. It is a symbol. The Great Architect "authored" the laws of nature that formed the universe and "willed" it into existence. The Great Architect is a symbol of the *how* and *why* of the universe. One can be learned, the other only speculated. *How* the universe was formed is revealed by science. *Why* is a mystery for philosophy. By learning how we are, we can imagine how we were, and know how far we've come. Wondering *why* we are here, we can imagine how we ought to be and know how far we have to go.

Since the nineteenth century the search for truth is increasingly scientific and less philosophical. This largely only concerns *how*. We know, in great detail, how the universe took shape, however we can venture no guess as to *why* it happened. Some reject the question. For them, there is no why; everything just is.

Any parent who ever entertained a curious toddler through a series of "why" questions understands such a routine can and will only stop when a stop is put to it. At a certain point, the answer for why anything is will be *it just is*. Sooner or later, the next answer will be one that either

---

* The Grand Orient of France removed the faith requirement in 1877.

the questioner can't understand or the answerer can't know. For most people this happens way before any talk of quantum mechanics or astrophysics, but even expert physicists will eventually arrive at the unanswerable. When your precocious three-year-old finally gets around to asking *why* the laws of thermodynamics exist, nobody is going to give a better answer than *they just do*. The kabbalist might prolong the game one more turn by

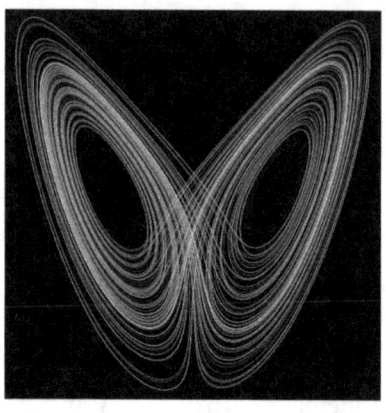

The "butterfly" pattern has become a symbol of chaos theory, illustrating how a small event in one area can have a large effect in a connected one.

attributing the laws to God. Nevertheless, ask *why* just once more and the white flag goes up. Why does God want it that way? He just does.

A proper kabbalist would never presume to know the will of God, and so from either perspective the first cause is unknown. However, there's a difference between Kabbalah's symbols of *divine will* as a first cause and the refusal of some to concede that there is a first cause at all. The kabbalists are free to wonder why they exist and the other group are not. To the unbeliever, there is no reason; the world just is. To the believer, the reason is a secret, perhaps to be discovered, perhaps not. In the end, neither knows why the world exists, but one is not allowed to wonder about it. So Masonry, like Kabbalah, maintains the mystery of a divine secret.

Secrecy and hidden mysteries

With mysterious imagery abounding in Kabbalah, terms like *secret* and *hidden* are easily subsumed under the general idea of the *unknown*.*
However the two concepts are not identical. The difference between

---

* To say nothing of the great impact of translation.

secret and unknown, if subtle, is significant. Even the best kept secret is *not* entirely unknown. Those keeping the secret know it. Something truly unknown isn't really secret. A secret is known by some and kept from others. It can be told, but isn't. Some secrets aren't told yet, some aren't told to everybody, and some are never told to anybody.

Freemasonry's relationship with secrecy is complicated. On one hand, secrecy is a calling card of the fraternity. What little the public knows about the group, it knows masons have secrets. This long-standing reputation is both beneficial and cumbersome. It accounts for any mystique which may remain around the group, as well as any suspicion. Among members themselves, on the other hand, there is almost no surviving opinion as to *why* masons have secrets. The exoteric explanations are obsolete, and no longer convincing, even to masons. With masonic exposés having long ago made public virtually all of the masonic ritual, passwords, and handshakes, it has become common for masons to say, almost confessingly, that there are, in fact, no secrets in Masonry.

To say, however, there are no secrets in Masonry is perhaps to speak too soon. A current willingness to do so suggests secrecy is no longer highly valued by many masons. Few masons can explain why they have secrets and most ultimately conclude there is no good reason. To be fair, it's unlikely any of them were ever given a good explanation themselves. Secrecy, like the tools of Freemasonry, is not practical, but is itself symbolic. A mason maintains this *overt* secrecy as a rich and multi-layered symbol.

First, masonic secrecy symbolizes the greater secrecy already mentioned: the concealed divine will. Simply put, Masonry has secrets because the world it tries to reflect has secrets. Second, it's specifically emblematic of the mystery each mason is personally pursuing. The goal of the masonic quest for light, the truth which has not yet been revealed and is still secret. Thirdly, on a practical level, masons keep secrets, as a symbol of their own trustworthiness. In real life, a mason can be counted on, not just to lend a hand to help, but also an ear to listen, a shoulder to lean on, or a heart in which to confide. Masons keep secrets to symbolize all this. The actual substance of those secrets may be of minor importance.

As tools, secrets are useful for masons. This includes keeping the ones they have and seeking answers to the ones they don't. It's similar to competitors or performers who set perfection as the goal of their training. They know perfection can never be achieved and will always be there to inspire them. They never arrive at perfection, but there is constant improvement and constant inspiration. In the same way, an ever-mysterious secret inspires us to keep exploring. Those who believe they know the secret, or that there is no secret, stop looking. Only people with questions look for answers. Replacing each revealed answer with the greater questions that lie behind it, they are forever engaged in the work at hand, and the adventure continues. That adventure is life. Believing there is always more out there than you know, and those things that are not real right now can become real someday, is an essential portion of hope.

The symbol of a divine Bride and Bridegroom, representing the marriage of above and below, is central
to Kabbalah and prominent in alchemical, particularly, Rosicrucian, symbolism.

CHAPTER 4

Existence and Perfection

To be or not to be

Earlier I proposed three simple tenets that would be agreeable to everybody. The first and simplest of these is the universe exists. This one is so obvious and unavoidable, it's easily taken for granted. Everyone agrees that we ourselves, along with the world around us, exist. Existence, however, is a multi-faceted enigma. Because nobody can be certain, there are a large variety of opinions about what it means to exist and why we, or anything, even exists at all. Why is something here instead of nothing? This question, asked by Gottfried Wilhelm Leibniz in the seventeenth century, may never be answerable. The unknown reason—the "will" or "impulse" behind existence, the undiscovered "cause" of the Big Bang—if not knowable, can still be the object of speculation. We can talk about it. We can wonder about it. Although no one can truly imagine the preexistent state of the world, let alone prove anything about it, few will deny that such was reality. It was just a reality we can't picture. Though it seems unlikely the universe will ever give up these secrets, much of what is true about the universe is also unlikely, including the fact that we exist at all.

Despite the profound mystery surrounding existence, people seem to agree that existing, at least when we are talking about ourselves, is better than *not* existing. In general, that is, we align with Shakespeare's *Hamlet*; we prefer *to be* over *not to be*. What it means to *exist*, to *be*, is still an open question. Hamlet, of course, meant by this *to live*. Existing, it must be confessed, is different from living. Plenty exists that doesn't actually live. Life is a special *type* of existence that is experienced and interpreted. A boulder simply exists, human beings live. We are aware of ourselves and things around us. We participate in our existence. So the moral teachings of Masonry first concern the questions of how *to be*, as Hamlet meant it, that is, how to live.

Existence however, even life, is more than just that of any one individual. Freemasonry, correspondingly, is more than a school of morality. Its teachings touch upon all of existence—past, present, and future. This is not only philosophical speculation, it's a practical concern. Traditions and history come from the past, morality and charity belong to the present, and the improvements we hope to see in ourselves and our communities await in the future. Masons are reminded to consider not only what exists now, but also what was, and what *should and can be*.

The difficulty in defining existence isn't with tangible but intangible things. Do they exist? Learning English grammar as a child, I was taught about nouns. A noun, as first explained to me in grade school, is a person, place, or thing. Nouns exist. People, places, and things exist. These are the easy ones. They literally occupy space and can be seen and touched. As I got a little older teachers began defining nouns with a fourth type. A noun is a person, place, thing, or *idea*. Ideas are nouns, but do they exist? They don't occupy space and they can't be seen or touched. Still, most of us would probably stop short of saying ideas don't exist.

Most would agree, ideas exist. We all have them, talk about them, and hope to share them with others. There are great ideas and terrible ideas. Thoughts compel us and revolt us. Feelings affect us. Love and friendships provide the greatest joy and deepest pain. Hope, dreams, and thoughts, all exist. They just don't exist the way people, places, and things do. They don't exist spatially, but they do exist temporally. They exist in our experience.

Different from your ideas or my ideas, we treat some ideas as independent concepts existing on their own. This may sound strange, until you remember people often refer to ideas in such a way.

It's a bad idea to expect something for nothing.

It's a good idea to think ahead.

Neither of these examples refer to any person's specific good or bad idea, but both still refer to a specific idea. The idea of *getting something for nothing* is common. Many have had it occur to them, others have heard it, and some may have just read it for the first time. There are those who find the idea attractive and those who (like in our example) denounce it. The same is true for the idea of *thinking ahead*. We talk about some ideas, not as though they belong to any one person but rather as though each person interacts with it.

The human brain likes things in categories. When we encounter an object (or an idea), we don't just see an object—we also see the *type* of object it is. Definitions describe a type or class of object. Say, for example, we accept the following definition of a book: *a collection of pages, fastened along one side, usually encased between front and back covers*. The definition tells us about a specific type of object, in this case a book. It states the properties any object of that type *must* have along with those it *may* have, and the extent to which any of them are required or allowed.

This definition tells us a book must have pages and they must be bound together on one side. This is the standard an object must meet to be a book, as well as the limits it must not exceed. No pages? No book. A loose stack of paper? Still not a book. Bind them on one side, and you've got a book. But don't go too far. Bind them on two sides and you'll have a weird stack of paper, but it won't be a book. The definition also tells the qualities an object *may* have and to what extent. A book can, and normally will, have both a front and a back cover, but that is not a strict requirement. A book with no cover is still, by this definition, a book.

Every object corresponds to a definition describing the type of object it is. This understanding is both ancient and modern. Plato referred to

Marble inlay depicting Hermes Trismegistus on the floor of the Siena Cathedral in Italy.

these types as *forms*. In object-oriented computer programming, they are commonly called *classes*. Every book is a single example (or if you prefer computer terminology, an *instance*) of a type of object called a book. If your friend says, "I think a book is an excellent gift," they have no specific book in mind but the sentence is not ambiguous. The general idea of "a book" is understood from the definition. A definition tells the properties an object can have, but it may not give all the information you want or need. In our example, it tells us a book has pages, but not how many. If your friend instead says, "*This book* will make an excellent gift," it's clear they are not talking about just any book, but a specific book. An example of the object reveals exactly the properties it *does* have and in precisely what measure. *This book* has 232 pages.

The Square and Compass, Freemasonry's most recognizable emblem and most important symbols, are inherited from the remote past. Across centuries and cultures, they represent by various explanations those two facets of existence, the ideal and the real. The square symbolizes the real, what is. The compass represents the ideal, that is, what could be and—more precisely—what should be. Abstract ideas, however, are never popular beyond small circles of philosophers. Accordingly, the compass and square were popularly explained as symbols of heaven and earth, at once concealing and revealing their existential meanings.

Anciently, the earth was regarded as flat and square, an idea memorialized in the expression *the four corners of the earth*. Even today, for practical purposes the earth is "flattened" for the sake of maps or the benefits of building on level ground, and "squared" to correspond to the four directions of north, south, east, and west. The square, a tool used by builders to ensure right angles, was a natural symbol of the flat, square earth. The compass, used to draw circles and arcs, represented the heavens, which appear to form a domed canopy over the earth. Together, the square and compass are a symbol of all existence, the ideal heavens and the real earth. Heaven doesn't refer to the sky or a far-off place, but is a symbol of ideas themselves. It is a symbol of perfection and permanence, an everlasting model of everything that could and should be. Earth, correspondingly, symbolizes what's real and actual. Limited in time and space, imperfect and temporary, but substantial and tangible.

Kabbalah similarly uses the symbols of heaven and earth, to represent the ideal and the real. Heaven, often called the *World Above*, is the ideal, the perfect prototype for Earth, which is the *World Below*. If you are acquainted with the Greco-Egyptian character Hermes Trismegistus, this may have a familiar ring. The most famous maxim attributed to his legend, *as above, so below*, is fundamental to Freemasonry and has a home in various religious and philosophical systems. Found encoded in scripture across the world's traditions, such universal concord is likely due to the plain simplicity of its truth. As above, so below. The idea is the blueprint for reality.

No type of advancement or success exists without there first being the idea of it. There can be no improvement, without the idea that conditions should improve. There can be no progress without a goal or target. The importance of recognizing this is crucial. The idea determines reality. This is not a "mind over matter" belief that the laws of nature can be overcome by psychic powers. It's a recognition that improvement can and will only happen when—and only to the degree which—there is a desire for it and a plan to achieve it. From high ideals comes the chance for exalted realities.

Perfection, Potential, and Truth

The idea that we can improve ourselves, and by doing so, improve the world, is at the heart of both Masonry and Kabbalah. *Be the change you wish to see in the world.* This famously simplified paraphrase of Mahatma Gandhi—though not what he actually said—conveys a valuable practical message.* If it's naive to suggest that a single person can "change" the world, as perhaps it is, it's nonetheless ungenerous to dispute that being kind results in more kindness. To think any act of kindness is so small it lacks significance, is a sad underestimation and ignores the laws of cause and effect. We can never know the total impact of every action we take, we can only know that the chain of causes and effects goes on forever, far beyond our ability to appreciate them.

So freemasons desire to improve, in the first place, themselves. Masons refer to the particular type of personal improvement that involves ridding oneself of vice and bad habits, as the act of *perfection*. This should not imply masons believe any of them can become a "perfect" person, but rather that they recognize the process of perfection continues through life. The first step in perfection, is necessarily, to identify imperfection. This requires accurate and regular assessment of one's self. Masons ought to be honest with all people, but first and foremost, they must be so with themselves.

Along with internal refinement, the aim of every mason should be to improve conditions wherever able, for their own benefit as well as that of their families and communities. The belief that things *should* be better is the earliest seed of charity—which is brotherly love. It starts with the

---

* What Gandhi actually said was: "We but mirror the world. All the tendencies present in the outer world are to be found in the world of our body. If we could change ourselves, the tendencies in the world would also change. As a man changes his own nature, so does the attitude of the world change towards him. This is the divine mystery supreme. A wonderful thing it is and the source of our happiness. We need not wait to see what others do."

simple recognition that life includes negative experiences—pain, fear, frustration—and is improved when those are made fewer or removed. The wish to see things improve for ourselves and families, is a preference that requires no explanation. Seeking improvement in our own lives is the work of perfecting ourselves. Seeking it in the lives of others is charity. To see suffering, pain, and trouble in the lives of people around you, and to believe those things call for relief, is to take a charitable view of others.

Whatever your goal or ambition, believing it's possible, allows for hope. Regardless of the problem, if I don't believe a solution is realistically possible, I have no hope. Imagine an overmatched basketball team trailing by twenty points with thirty seconds left in a game. They have a problem, but there is a solution. If they hit seven three-pointers, one every four seconds, and don't give up any more points to the other team, they can win. All the players understand what has to happen. However, none of them believe it's possible. They have no hope.

Hope believes that what we want to happen, can happen. Once there's hope, the further belief that what's hoped for *will happen*, is faith. Faith is, therefore, the culmination of the others: *charity*, the belief that things should improve, *hope*, the belief that they can improve, and *faith*, the belief that they will improve. Without faith, the first two are irredeemable. What value can there be in believing something should happen, and could happen, but won't? Of the three, faith is also the most fleeting. It applies only to those things which are possible but not real. Anything falling beyond those boundaries, becoming impossible on one hand, or entirely real on the other, is no longer an object of faith.

You may recognize the reference to the New Testament where Paul writes: "*And now abideth faith, hope, charity, these three; but the greatest of these is charity.*" (*1 Corinthians 13:13*) I selected this translation, the King James Version, produced in 1611, for the classic rendering of the word *charity*. Most modern translations render the Greek word *agape* as *love*. Charity, particularly as it was then used, does not specifically mean giving money to the less fortunate, although it might still have taken that form. It is, rather, a charitable spirit toward others. A feeling that generously produces unconditional kind regard for each person and wishes the best for all. It is called "the greatest" of the three. One reason is because it supports the other two and sets hope and faith on a noble foundation of brotherly love. It is also the most permanent of the three. Belief in what *can* or *will* be, ends when it becomes real. However, what is or isn't, has no impact on your beliefs about what *should* be.

Faith, hope, and charity are parts of a larger symbol in Masonry. When considered as just explained, they are steps in the search for truth. For a freemason, or any other person, the search for truth can be a difficult thing to explain. It's not like trying to find lost car keys. Humans experience the truth both really and ideally. In one case, there is the truth as it is right now. All of the measurable facts of the world; the truth of the present; what *is*. This expression of the truth is the most useful to us, and often the most satisfying, but ultimately the least perfect. It's the most practical for obvious reasons. Being aware of facts allows us to make informed decisions. However, the present truth is not perfect. It is temporary. It is true right now, but may not have been true yesterday and may not be true tomorrow.

What may be true tomorrow, that is, *potential*, is a different truth. We don't deny that potential is true—potential energy, for example, is a well-established scientific concept. We understand that, if conditions change, the truth will change as well. Potential can become actual. But what about potential that isn't realized? How we view unrealized potential, depends on two things. First, whether it was thought to be good or bad, and second, whether it waits in the future or lurks in the past. Unrealized *bad* potential, if in the past, is *fortuity*, something negative that could have happened but didn't. In the future, something bad that could happen but hasn't, is *danger*. Conversely, something *good* that could have happened but didn't—unrealized *good* potential from the past—is *regret*. Something good that could happen in the future but hasn't yet is *hope*.

	Good	Bad
Past	Regret	Fortuity
Future	Hope	Fear

How we think of unrealized potential

Conditions constantly change, and potential is made actual. The truth that *could be* becomes the truth *that is*, and a new potential awaits. Potential is also temporary, it doesn't wait forever. For good or bad, potential can disappear. For every unfulfilled hope, there is a danger safely bypassed. What is possible right now will not always be possible. Like any idea of perfection, the perfect truth is an idea that can never be realized. The Truth that has always been true and will always be true—eternal, infinite, and perfect—is, somewhat ironically, unknowable. It is not the truth of the past, present, or future, nor is it the truth of the matter. It is the Truth that precedes matter and exists apart from time.

Returning to practical terms, consider the historical four-minute-mile run by Roger Bannister in 1954. Prior to this, some believed the limit of a human's ability to run a mile was just above four minutes. Running is among the oldest human activities. The fact that a faster time had never been recorded, was, for many, reasonably convincing evidence that a faster time was not possible. At the time, the truth of the matter was no human, though many had tried, could break the limit of four minutes.

That changed on May 6, 1954 when Roger Bannister ran a mile in under four minutes. What seemed a true limit the day before, was not true anymore. A new truth was revealed, which itself, was not the perfect truth, but was a tiny bit closer. The limit was not four minutes—the world now knew that—but what was it? What is it? Bannister's time didn't stand for long. The record was broken and reset several times within months of his historic first time. At the time of this writing, the world record for the mile is 3:43, set in 1999. This record has stood now for twenty-five years. Is this the limit to human ability? Of course that is doubtful. It's reasonable to think somebody will come along and break this barrier too. But what if nobody does? And even if somebody does break it, and someone else breaks their record after that, it can't go on like that forever. There must be an actual limit to how fast a human being can run a mile. Can a human run a mile in 3:40? Probably. 3:30? Maybe. Two minutes? Probably not. Thirty seconds? No. Definitely not.

Shown here in 1953, future neurologist and history making runner, Roger Bannister proved a human could run a mile in under four minutes.

There is a limit to how fast a human being can run a mile. That is the truth. There's just no way to know what that limit is. It's not a magical number, however, the calculation required to predict it is unimaginably complex. Whatever the number might be, the true limit was set by the laws of nature, billions of years before the first person ever ran a step. If nobody ever actually achieves it, it will still always be the true limit. This is the perfect truth, impervious to time and, to us, unknowable. However it is constantly being approached and approximated, ever more closely and accurately. Every newly revealed state, though imperfect, is an improved image of perfection. The three steps of charity, hope, and faith, symbolically traverse the space between the imperfect state from which we begin, and the perfected state to which masons hope to bring themselves and the world around them.

Charity, or brotherly love, recognizes the imperfect state—*the truth that is*—and believes change should happen. Hope sees potential—*the truth that can be*—and adds the belief that what should happen, can happen. Faith doesn't see, it believes. Called blind, faith doesn't have its eyes closed, but it looks forward to the unknowable future. It believes simply and logically the ultimate truth is undeniable—it can never be made untrue—and what should be, eventually will be. This is the truth which has always been, the eternal Truth, symbolized by freemasons as the *plans drawn* by the Great Architect of the Universe. The belief in such a Truth is foundational to the work of Freemasonry.

A belief that the way things are is not how they should be implies there is a way they should be. Should be according to who or what? What should or ought to happen, describes an intended or expected outcome. Without intention or expectation, there is nothing that "should" be, only what is. So masons maintain the idea that conditions *should* be better, that suffering *should* be relieved, and that improvements *should* be made. This is, symbolically, the Great Architect's plan. Their work and hope is to bring reality closer to that ideal. They seek this progress by improving themselves, providing support for their families and communities, and relieving the distressed. The connection between how things are and how they should be, is one layer of symbolic meaning reflected in the union of the square and the compass.

Space and Time

If this sounds like the stuff of daydreams, it is more practical than that. Albert Einstein's (1879–1955) theories of Special and General Relativity changed our understanding of physics in the early part of the twentieth century. Since then, a great deal has been learned about the special relationship between time and space. Of primary significance, space and time are not actually two separate things but are distinct aspects of *spacetime*, a single, mysterious fabric supporting everything in the known universe. The ideas of spacetime relativity are not intuitive. Apart from astrophysicists, even bright, well-educated people, find the concepts difficult to explain and understand. For the purposes of this book, there is only so much benefit that can be had from the discussion of spacetime. Therefore, space and time are considered practically, in a way familiar to human experience, and it will be enough in most cases simply to acknowledge the greater truth that space and time are connected in strange and mysterious ways.

Space is the *where* and *how much* of existence. Existing in space means occupying a finite amount of it and a unique position in relation to all other things. More simply, everything has a size and shape and everything has a place (something my wife has been reminding me since 1997). Volume and dimensions, distance, position, and angles, are measures of space. Space—that is, physical existence—is intuitive; we understand it naturally and well. In fact, some people understand it very well. The field of physics, starting with Newton, has shaped the modern understanding of the world beyond what anyone could once imagine. The human grasp of physical reality, allows us to build ever greater machines and buildings, put satellites into orbit around the earth, and advance medicine and technology in astounding ways. Time, however, is different. It's an elusive construct and humans can't quite put our finger on it exactly. As familiar as it seems to every person, we don't really know what time is. We experience it as a fourth dimension of reality. In its simplest reckoning, time is the progression from the past to the future. But both the past and the future are ideal. The past is a memory and the future is imagination. They don't exist in reality, at least, not as far as we can be aware.

As impossible as time is to understand, it's just as impossible to imagine a world where nothing ever changed or moved. Change is a difference between two points in time. Life is experienced as change and movement. Things grow and shrink, come together or spread apart, but only in time. Improvement is change, and determining where change is needed requires comparing reality to an ideal. We compare our state now with the state we want in the future to determine how far we have to go. We measure against our past state to see how far we've come. Looking forward gives us hope and aspirations. Looking behind us gives perspective and confidence. The lifelong experience of a person involved in self-improvement or charity consists of measuring reality and moving it ever closer to an ideal.

For this reason Masonry, with its symbolic connection to ancient builders, includes many different types of tools as symbols. Some tools, a hammer and chisel for example, are applied to the building material for effect. They are intended to change the size or shape of the stone. Other tools are employed to assess the condition of the material. They show how much change has happened and how much is still needed. They are used to test or measure. The square is such a tool. Placed against the stone, it indicates if the stone is right and, if the stone is not, where and how much correction is needed. The process of improvement involves accurate assessment followed by measured and directed change.

Using practical tools as symbols admits a sublayer of meaning. Whatever the tool, if it is to provide any benefit at all, it has to be used. Having a hammer and chisel in your toolbox doesn't get a cathedral built. A tool is only valuable in the hand of a worker who knows how to use it and, most importantly, actually does. It's a symbolic reminder that whatever usefulness any instrument may provide, it's not the tool but the builder who does the work. A tool is worthless if it is not used and potentially harmful if not used correctly.

A stonemason using a hammer and chisel. Notice the square on the table.

Desolate Helgoland island where Werner Heisenburg conceived quantum mechanics in 1925.

CHAPTER 5

In the Beginning

After agreeing we exist, the second point upon which all can agree, is, we didn't always exist. The world, in the unimaginably distant past, had a beginning, before which there was, as far as either scientists or philosophers can guess, nothing. The specific details of what brought everything from nothing, the unknown first cause, people disagree about. Nobody, however, suggests it didn't happen. The world is here now. It wasn't always. Something happened, but nobody can say for sure what it was or why it happened. The result was the Big Bang—the Beginning—and the birth of everything that now exists; time and space, matter and energy.

Ein Sof, Nothing, and Professor Stephen Hawking

Long before any inkling of spacetime or the Big Bang, ancient philosophers concluded there must have been a first cause. Over centuries the idea was expanded and developed by the greatest Greek and Arab philosophers. In the Middle Ages, these thinkers inspired Jewish philosophers, setting the stage for the ideological challenges brought by Maimonides's rational school against the popular faith.

Beginning in ancient times, rabbis maintained the customs and traditions of Judaism. This job was, over time, made increasingly difficult by ever growing religious competition and hostility. In the Middle Ages, internal criticism from a respected voice, was almost too much to bear. The rabbis who made it their duty to defend tradition, had no choice but to respond. The nature of the criticism was direct. The popular faith was replete with myths and legends which were indefensible by rationalist thinking. The task assumed by the early kabbalists was not simple: to integrate contemporary concepts into the traditional stories of the Bible.

The philosophers, for their part, could not budge on the issue. Rationalism simply wouldn't tolerate the illogic and frequent paradox so common to folk tradition. All the distance between religion and philosophy would have to be traversed by Kabbalah. The traditional symbols would have to be reexplained in ways that satisfied contemporary thinking. The symbols, however, were the written words of the Bible, the holy writings often referred to as *the Law*. If the logic of philosophers was uncompromising, tradition was "set in stone" so to speak. Neither the words of the Bible nor centuries of ritualized observance could be changed in the slightest. The same old words would, somehow, have to acquire new meaning.

The rationalist view of divinity couldn't admit even the slightest limit or deficiency. Philosophers, therefore, carefully avoided any description which could be interpreted to fall short of perfection. This led to *negative theology*, where no qualities are positively attributed to deity. The Divine is only describable in terms of what it *is not* or *cannot be*. God has no beginning and no end, God cannot be described by words, etc. Taken to its final and possibly unavoidable conclusion, God eventually is described as *nothing* or, as some enjoy saying, *no thing*. Perhaps pleasing to the intellectual mind, "God is nothing" was then, as it still is, strange to the religious ear.

Philosophers, as the fate of Socrates attests, have never been exceedingly popular.* Societies, it appears, have always inclined more to the comfort and kinship in folklore and superstition than the cold and barren frontier of rationalism. Hence, a broad variety of gods and deities were produced by early civilizations. The populations who revered and worshiped these gods tended to envision them in the forms of persons. Perhaps embellished

---

* Socrates was sentenced to exile or death for "corrupting the youth" with his ideas. He chose death.

with extraordinary features, divine beings generally portrayed human qualities and experienced human emotions. These gods were also imagined to have personal interactions with people and nature, intervening in the lives of mortals, responding to them and providing for them.

The impersonal god conceived by philosophers, was difficult, if not impossible, for people to embrace. A deity completely unconcerned with human activity—or reduced to nothing—did little to comfort or inspire hope. Kabbalists provided an answer. *Ein Sof*, a Hebrew phrase that means *without end*, became a symbol of the transcendent god of the philosophers. The *unknowable* god, it was imagined, desired to reveal itself. In a series of emanations issuing from the hidden essence of Ein Sof, the God of tradition—who answers prayers and "dwells" with the people—is *revealed*. These emanations, the *sephirot*, start with *Keter*, God's unfathomable *Will*, called, among other nicknames, *ayin*, nothing.

Having successfully made something from the philosopher's "nothing," the kabbalists of the twelfth century seemed to anticipate one of the most celebrated minds of modern science. "*I believe the Universe created itself out of nothing according to the laws of nature.*"[17] These words were penned by astrophysicist Stephen Hawking and published in 2018. This statement, by a dogged scientist and presumed atheist, was meant to explain his disbelief in God (at least his disagreement with the common definition of God). However, with it the late Dr. Hawking, unsuspecting kabbalist he apparently was, provided a line which, translated into the language of Kabbalah, might be completely at home on the pages of the *Zohar*.

Replace the phrase "laws of nature" with "Law of God" and the same idea is expressed spiritually. *I believe the Universe created itself out of nothing according to the Law of God.* However, to say "the Universe created itself" produces a logical problem. A song can't write itself and the Universe can't create itself. For kabbalists, as may soon be clear, such logical roadblocks are hardly daunting.

According to Kabbalah, the reason for Creation is the desire of the hidden *Ein Sof* to reveal itself. This revelation begins with the emanation of the first of the sephirot, Keter, also called *ayin, nothing*. The Hebrew word for universe, *olam*, also means "infinity" and "eternity." To kabbalists, Dr. Hawking would have simply been stating something the sages had always known. He may as well have said, "*I believe Ein Sof revealed itself out of divine Will, according to the Law of God.*

What may seem to be a dodge, or simply clever word play, is actually more substantial. There is an important concept brought forward in this, my hypothetical example. Creation is synonymous with divine *revelation.* The creative process begins with the unknowable wishing to be knowable. *Ein Sof's* infinite nature makes it inconceivable. However, the *sephirot* are finite. Each reveals specific qualities of divinity which are comprehensible to humans. The attributes of divinity become knowable in creation while the true essence of divine nature remains hidden. The self-revealed Godhead provides the blueprint for the material world. The entire universe is a reflection of divinity and the created world is patterned after the emanated world.

Another kabbalistic tenet is that creation, the process of revelation, unfolded according to a divine plan, recorded before time, in the *Torah.* Torah is the Hebrew word for "teaching" and is the common name given to the Bible. In this context, it is often known as "the Law."* The Torah—the writings of which are central to Judeo-Christian belief—is, for kabbalists, not simply a collection of holy scriptures. Like the mysterious *Tao* of Lao Tzu, of which is said "*the Tao that can be written is not the eternal Tao*," the written words of Torah are not the complete Torah.[18] Torah is the divine Truth, the Law of God, and can only be partially revealed in scripture. Along with what's written, there is an *Oral Torah*, which was passed only from mouth to ear for generations. However, even these two together don't tell the complete story of the Torah. The *true* Torah is the *Sacred Law,* which is continuously revealed in creation by the endless forms in which we recognize *Truth,* everywhere that it's found.

The *Holy Bible* or the *Volume of the Sacred Law,* as it's called by freemasons, is a symbol of the laws that govern the universe. It's present

---

* The Septuagint often translates the Hebrew *torah* with the Greek *nomos*; Exodus 12:49 for example. In the New Testament, this word is used when the Hebrew scriptures are referred to as "the Law and the Prophets."

in every regular lodge representing the masonic belief that the Great Architect of the Universe may be known, and thereby present among us, through the observation of nature and the laws of the universe. From one masonic jurisdiction to another, and for individual masons of different faiths, the book may change but the symbolic meaning is not affected. The book, whichever one it is, is a symbol of the laws of nature by which the world was created and is sustained.

It's about time

To speak of the beginning of the Universe, or the beginning of anything, is necessarily, to acknowledge time. As was said in the last chapter, time is a mystery as enigmatic as existence itself, and similarly something often taken for granted. That isn't to say humans aren't aware of time, we certainly are. We are aware of our own mortality and that our existence is only for a finite time, and we are aware that time is passing with the hours, days, and seasons. But, in the same way that we *can* appreciate light because we understand darkness, perhaps time is so easily overlooked because, conversely, it's so difficult, if not impossible, to imagine existence *without* it. A world without time would be a world without movement. Entirely static, unmoving, unchanging, completely dark, cold, and silent (light, heat, and sound have to travel), devoid of even the simplest forms of life and thought.

As obviously essential as time is to existence, and as strange as it may seem, there was a "time" before time. The Big Bang occurred in a state of reality into which time was yet to be introduced. It's been said that asking what existed "before" the Big Bang is like asking what lies south of the South Pole.[†] Time starts at the Beginning. Asking what was "before" it, as natural as it seems, actually doesn't make sense. So why do we have time? Why does existence occur in time? This question, for now, gets the same answer as asking why anything exists at all. It just does, which in

† The so-called "no-boundary" theory of Stephen Hawking and James Hartle.

Kabbalah, is another way of saying it's divine will. God just wanted it that way. But if we agree that the universe had a beginning and, although we don't like to think about it, has an inevitable end, and if we are allowed to imagine that creation accords to a plan, and the final fate of the world though unknown to us has forever been determined, then it begs the question, why the long process? Why didn't God just create the world in its finalized state? Of course, an answer can only be imagined, but when we contemplate this question we realize that time, whatever the reason that we have it, is a gift. For masons time is also a symbol.

Time, as was discussed, allows for change, without which there is neither growth nor improvement. Each person records in their memory how they felt and what they sensed and thought during certain spans of their lifetime. This is what we call experience. Human life occurs within a finite amount of time, during which we experience the world, while both we and it constantly change. Our identities and lives are the product of the accumulation of our experiences. Most of us can probably think of our own childhood, and note several differences between our current self and our many former versions. Each step in your development led to the person you are and the life you've lived up to this point.

Now imagine that you had just emerged, fully formed, like the Greek goddess Athena from the mind of Zeus. Possessing all the information an adult would have accumulated through childhood, without experiencing any of it. What would you know about such wonderful and important things like childish wonder, puppy love, teenage heartache, adolescent angst, or any of the fantastic idealism of youth? What would you think of yourself? Could there be any idea of accomplishment or regret? Could you feel the sense of satisfaction that should accompany a well spent life? Besides such things being difficult to imagine, they don't sound particularly appealing. Fortunately for us, life is not like this. Experience builds on previous experience, understanding is augmented, and growth and progress are incremental. Time elapsing gradually as it does, allows for much greater learning and provides richness and layers to our knowledge.

Masonry represents this condition of human existence in certain symbolic tools and in the gradual advancement through its several degrees. The fourth dimension, time, whether a cosmic accident, or a thoughtful gift to mankind, is emblematized by the beginning, middle, and end of the masonic journey delineated by the stepwise process. Borrowing from the Bible story of creation, each mason's *beginning* is the introduction of *light* against symbolic *darkness*. Much of the symbolism we'll explore is taken from the creation account in Genesis, familiar for its famous first declaration, "In the Beginning, God created the Heavens and the Earth" and the vivific fiat that soon follows, "Let there be light."[19]

As the story goes, after God "created the Heavens and the Earth," the Earth was still unformed.[20] Creation should be thought of, not as a single act, but as an ongoing event. Immediately after the initial creative movement, starting with the introduction of light, a process ensued over a period which lasted, depending on your source, between seven days and several billion years. By whichever interpretation, we see symbolically that everything, from the beginning, exists in time as well as space. Masons are reminded to make the most of their time, organize it, and use it industriously. Though their own allotment of time is finite, they can be patient, understanding things must occur in due course.

Whatever happened at the Beginning, whether it took a matter of days or eons, it's long over now. That is, we think of the creation of the universe as something that happened a long time ago, not something that is still happening. Kabbalah presents a different perspective. The act of creation, as kabbalists explain, is not simply an event that happened long ago—it's a process that continues even today and must not be interrupted. Creation is ongoing. It's essentially another word for existence. Should the creative process be disturbed, the entire universe would stop existing! The story of creation, more than the most important theme of Kabbalah, might be said to be the only theme. Every story of the Bible is, when viewed through this lens, a story of creation, concerning not just the first creative event but the continuing maintenance of the universe.

Kabbalists imagined the *sephirot* forming a divine apparatus by which the flow of life and the blessings of heaven pass from above to below. The paths connecting them were envisioned as conduits for the delivery of spiritual substance across the ten spheres and eventually to the physical world. This network also transmits from below to above. Prayers and charitable acts of mankind, enhance the flow of divinity. On the other hand, selfish and vicious behavior disrupts the stream of providence. The divine pathways become polluted, further obstructing the world-preserving flow and placing all of existence in peril.

Step by step

At this dramatic point in the story, it must be made explicit nothing about the *sephirot* should be imagined to exist literally. This is important to emphasize. Kabbalists don't believe in a quasi-physical network of semi-divine beings traversing space or any other arrangement by which the *sephirot* are anything other than symbols. The *sephirot* represent various concepts, each meant to provoke the contemplation of perfection by imagining a specific virtue in its most perfected state. These symbols are useful reminders and contemplative vehicles. The *sephirot* metaphorically link the ideal to the real by an intricate series of symbolic pathways. They can be figuratively climbed—elevating the individual toward perfection—or descended, bringing blessings and allowing Perfection and Truth, to be occasionally glimpsed.

The structured nature of the *sephirot* is also symbolic. They aren't loose or jumbled, they're orderly and arranged. This signifies that the world is not chaotic. The laws are consistent and produce a balanced and orderly system. This makes the world very predictable.* The laws of the universe don't change, regardless of time or place. Weightlessness experienced by humans while orbiting the Earth in outer space is not because there

---

* If earthquakes and unpredictable weather seem to contradict that, remember the world is also very complex. We have no way of collecting all the information needed to accurately predict weather. However, if we did, with supercomputers capable of performing the calculations, we could not only predict the weather perfectly every day, we could determine with perfect accuracy what the weather was like every day since the Earth was formed.

is, as we commonly hear, "no gravity" in space. That would be very far from the truth.[†] Gravity is, in fact, what's keeping spacecraft in orbit. The weightlessness is due to *how* gravity works. A characteristic of gravity is, its effect decreases the further two objects are from each other. The further a person is from the Earth, the less they feel the Earth's gravity. But gravity is still there and always works the same way. Experiment after experiment confirms this. Because we understand that the laws of nature are fixed and never change, we can reliably predict their effects anywhere and everywhere.[‡] The same laws allow us to build towers and bridges on Earth and to send satellites into orbit around our own planet and others.

The gradual arrangement of the *sephirot* also has symbolic meaning. Nothing comes into existence instantly. Everything starts as potential, manifests in a small way, and grows, through numerous influences, into what it eventually becomes. Even the universe did this. The emergence of the *sephirot* consecutively, reflects the gradual unfolding of existence. The directed and mediated flow of providence through the *sephirot*, symbolizes the varied influences underlying the complex and intricate nature of everything. Your life is the result of a process that began when the world began, and your present experience is the accumulation of your past experiences. You don't go to sleep one night as a child and wake up one day as an adult.[§] Your body and mind both develop by steps and, although every step is succeeded by the next, none is a wasted or unimportant step. Each contributes something that supports the next one and makes the value of the previous ones more appreciable.

Not only must blessings pour down, but the supplications of the people must be lifted up and their transgressions likewise registered. Acts of good and bad are conveyed heavenward via the *sephirot* and impact the delivery of divine providence to the world. This interchange between *Heaven* and *Earth* is not a quid pro quo system of reward and punishment, but signifies the value of cooperating with the laws that

---

[†] Gravity, it turns out, is an interaction, not between two objects but between matter and space.

[‡] ...or at least believe that the laws of nature don't change. We can't prove that. But if they are changing, they are doing it at a rate too slow for us to detect.

[§] Although it sometimes feels like that's exactly what happened.

govern the universe and the futility of opposing them. This ancient concept reflects early attempts to understand the universal laws of cause and effect. Eventually, Newton would explain that for every action there is an equal and opposite reaction.[21] Ancient civilizations believed much the same thing. However, they tended to assume the *reaction* might be supernatural.[22]

In Kabbalah the *sephirot* are frequently presented as a symbolic *ladder*. During prayer or meditation they lead ever closer to the Divine. This symbol will also be familiar to masons. Progress is not just growth. Adults are more than just big children. There is an accumulation of ideas and a refinement of practices that constitute personal development. Some qualities are prerequisite for the development of others. The *sephirot* provide a conceptual road map where the approach to *wisdom* begins with a proper *foundation*, and the variety of paths, makes each journey a unique experience.[*]

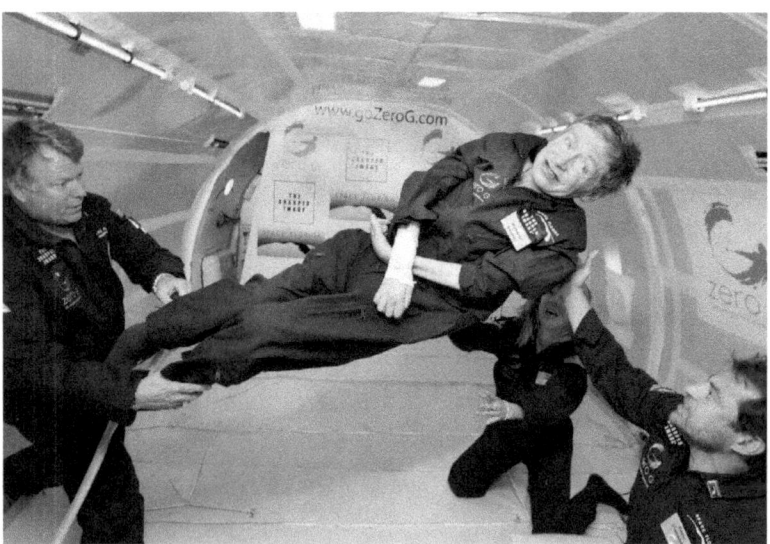

Dr. Stephen Hawking at the edge of Earth's gravitational pull.

---

[*] Going from bottom to top, the sephirah *Yesod*, foundation, is the first step above *Malkhut*. *Hokhmah*, wisdom, is the highest sephirah that can be contemplated, the only one higher being *Keter*, the most mysterious divine Will.

The metaphors of a *ladder* ascending ever higher, or a *journey* to a destination, are obvious symbols for self-improvement. Masonry and Kabbalah use both. The symbol of building is another representation of progress and development. Different from a journey, where what you did yesterday fades behind you, in a building, yesterday's work is present and must still be accounted for. Poor work yesterday, poor structure today. While we shouldn't dwell in the past, or stubbornly refuse to forgive ourselves or others, we have to be accountable for our actions. What we do—today and always—matters for ourselves and others.

The Long Arm of the Law

After agreeing already, that we exist and didn't always exist (i.e., the world had a beginning), the third point we can agree upon is we exist according to *laws*. These laws are, as Spinoza put it, of "God or nature"[23] and are present from the farthest reaches of space to the deepest reveals of subatomic reality. As far as anybody can tell, laws of nature, such as gravity, are constant and consistent everywhere and at all times. They don't change. Of course, we have only been observing a relatively small portion of nature for a relatively short time. There's always a chance that some discovery in the future will change our minds about this. It wouldn't be the first time humanity underwent a massive shift in our fundamental beliefs about reality. Although another such shift will almost definitely happen again in the future, there's nothing to suggest that the known laws of nature are not, as we believe them to be, fixed and permanent in all places at all times.

Modern physicists, chemists, and mathematicians continue to discover ever more intricate and amazing features that literally define the world we live in. Many laws of the universe are already known to science and presumably many others will be discovered. Some of them, people relate to, like gravity. Many more are only known and grasped by a few experts in specialized pursuits. With impressive experiments and complicated mathematical formulas, scientists are achieving an understanding of the universe that is absolutely astounding. As human knowledge advances, the picture of reality may become more accurate, but that doesn't always mean it gets clearer. Answers lead to new questions and sometimes our entire view of reality is radically overthrown.

Humanity continues on a quest to understand the rules that govern our world. Our grasp of these laws *is* our relationship with the Truth. The early stages of this search, were limited by both the observations which could be made and the prevailing theories of the times. Ancient Greek philosophers, starting with Thales (c. 626–548 BCE), imagined all things to be, at their essence, made up of a single fundamental element. This may eventually turn out to be true.* However, with no ability to look more closely than with the naked eye, the first guesses at what it might be, were way off. Thales says the primary element is water. Anaximander (c. 610–546 BCE) later says it's air. Empedocles (c. 494–434 BCE) takes both and adds two of his own, earth and fire. Aristotle (384–322 BCE), not to be left out, adds a fifth element, ether, which pertains to stars and the features of heaven. That theory would more or less dominate Western thought for centuries.

The Swiss physician Paracelsus (1493–1541), never one to follow convention, adopted the more practical alchemical theory of Arabic chemist and magician Geber (Jabir ibn Hayyan). All metals, it was believed, were a mixture of mercury, sulfur, and arsenic. Ever the individual, Paracelsus replaced arsenic with salt and proposed his three "principles" of matter. All of these ideas were wrong, some cartoonish by modern standards. However, all were born from a belief in the same general truth: the many different things we see around us are, at their essence, made from the same basic ingredients. We still believe this. They tried then, as we still do now, to imagine what those essential building blocks might be and to discover them. Their handicaps, which were insurmountable, were placed directly against their genius, which was indomitable. Though they could never realize the truths they imagined, their early contributions paved the path for those who would.

---

* Superstring theory

Of course, human achievement in terms of knowledge, from the times of Paracelsus and natural philosophy, has been astounding. Newton's description of the physical world, given in 1687, was the blueprint for reality for almost three hundred years and, in many ways, still is. However, as the true scientist and absolutely monumental intellect he was, Newton was troubled by the gaps in his knowledge that were later filled in by Einstein. Newton could prove gravity worked exactly as he believed, he just didn't know why.[24] His assumptions about the nature of space were eventually overturned by Einstein's Special Relativity. His discoveries concerning gravity were better explained by Einstein's subsequent theory of General Relativity.

Einstein would explain how gravity works, but relativity would not be the end of the story. We've come a remarkably long way from the days of four elements. We understand the world to be made up of molecules and atoms, and atoms to be made up of parts even smaller, and those parts to be made up of parts even smaller than those. As scientists have been able to get a better look at the building blocks of the universe, they've seen things they haven't been able to explain. Einstein's ideas worked great when you were talking about big things like buses and buildings and planets and stars. In fact, in those cases, they work perfectly. In experiment after experiment, relativity has never been wrong—until things got microscopically tiny. At the subatomic level, the predictions of relativity don't match what scientists observe. Another new idea was needed. It was provided by Werner Heisenberg (1901–1976) with quantum mechanics. This theory accounts as perfectly for the subatomic world as relativity does for the larger world we see.

Humans have dug deep into the mysteries of the world, uncovering more and more of the laws of the universe. These laws, in their essence, describe the rules governing the forces of the universe. With all of the action and motion of the world, it might be surprising to know that binding and propelling everything are only four forces. They consist of two that we encounter daily, gravitational force and electromagnetic force, and two that only apply at the atomic level, called the Strong Force and the Weak Force.[25] The point is what we call law, whether it's the law of man, God, or nature, consists of force applied appropriately within the bounds traced out by the rules that govern it. This is a most important symbol for freemasons.[26]

Law and Order

By contemplating these laws, we hope to know more about ourselves, our origins, and our true potential. To understand the world, was the motivation that inspired the ancients and is the same one that drives the modern search for truth. We're still engaged, as earnestly as we were then, in trying to understand the fundamental building blocks of existence and the rules that bind everything together. The quest for knowledge can be retraced back to the dawn of humanity. It's clear the ancient philosophers of Greece, Egypt, India, and China, didn't lack in logic, insight, or imagination. However, they hadn't the benefit of thousands of years of writing as the later Europeans of the Renaissance had. The conclusions they reached were based on the observable precision of the natural world.

Abrupt storms or natural disasters aside, the world acts in predictable ways. This is made possible by the constancy of the laws of nature. Because this is true, not only will the sun predictably rise tomorrow, but I already know what time that will happen. The features of nature behave consistently. The sea rises and falls according to the precise application of the moon's gravity and both fishermen and surfers in coastal towns pay careful attention to tide charts that predict these events perfectly. Water freezes and iron melts at the same temperatures every day.* The stars proceed through the sky in an annually repeating pattern. To the people of ancient civilizations, everything about the world suggested a natural order. Though they didn't know exactly how this order was accomplished, it was understood to indicate an idea of rightness. If order was how the

---

* Respectively, 0° C (32° F) and 1530° C (2786° F).

gods and nature conducted the world, then order was the right way and the opposite, chaos, was the wrong way.

Every representation of "the Law" symbolizes the order which a collection of rules is intended to provide. Order, at the risk of oversimplifying the point, is good. We benefit from it as individuals and as groups. Societies require it of their members and hope to provide a structure for them to achieve it. All of us, even the most impulsive, creative, or spontaneous free-spirit, require a certain amount of predictability in the world or it would be insane. We don't want life to be the movie *Groundhog Day*, where every day is exactly like the day before. However, when we go to bed at night we do expect that we'll wake up the next morning in the same world we went to sleep in. For the most part, this is what happens. The sun rises on time and the moon waxes and wanes. Nothing inexplicably appears or disappears. Things are predictable. Anything else would be chaotic.

Maintaining order in one's personal life, becomes a symbol of the natural order that makes life enjoyable and which is a true gift. In the arrangement of their own time and space masons should hope to reflect that order found in nature, which is a model for, country, community, family, and self. Order is provided by the laws that marshal each one. There are the civil laws that govern your relationship with your community, and the moral law that governs your relationship with yourself and others. To strive and desire, for our institutions and persons, to display the sort of perfection that we observe in the laws of God or nature, is what masons are reminded each time we're called to order. To bring order, whenever possible, to our lodges and their operation, and at all times, to our own health and thoughts, as well as to our conduct and affairs.

We often think of order specifically in terms of progression. Things are arranged in numerical or alphabetical *order*. By this understanding, order symbolizes the rightness of things occurring in the correct sequence. This is how nature works and is portrayed symbolically in Masonry. It's reflected in the gradual promotion of members by degree and in the progressive advance of lodge officers "through the chairs" to increasingly higher stations. A person can't expect to develop by receiving an unordered assemblage of facts and theories. Everything must be applied, not just in progressive steps, but in the right order.

It's really not so simple

It might seem our knowledge would clear things up and lead to a simple understanding of the truth. That is, however, far from the case. The theories we rely on to explain the world, explain a very strange place. Einstein tells us that space and time are relative. Quantum mechanics gives us uncertainty theory. None of these things are intuitive to us. We are far too big and slow for the strangeness of either relativity or quantum physics to ever appear in our lives. The truth is that the Truth, beyond what we can see, is exceedingly different from the world that we experience every day. However, we're not separated from it. The objects of the real world are the products of these unseen forces that obey mysterious rules which sometimes seem to contradict our natural understanding of how things work.

The world is complex and fascinating. It's not easy to understand. Nobody has completely figured it out, and it's not likely anyone ever will. The more we look, the more we find mystery at the bottom of everything. Solving any unknown, uncovers new and deeper unknowns. While some may find unsettling the notion that true certainty is ultimately impossible, others find the prospect of a never-ending quest to be exhilarating. It means there will always be questions to ask and answers to seek. The great scientific advances of the twentieth and twenty-first centuries have brought us not just plenty of answers, but plenty of new questions as well. The "Holy Grail" of current science may be the so-called "unified theory" or "theory of everything," a single theory that accounts for the gaps and incompatibilities in our current knowledge. As mentioned, the leading theories for explaining the world, relativity and quantum mechanics, are at odds with each other. They can't both be right. The strange world can sometimes make it difficult to know what to believe. This is part of humanity's search for truth, what freemasons symbolically call the search for *light*.

Scientists will keep up the search. We can be certain of that. Perhaps fittingly, a front-running proposal as a unified theory is called by the mysterious name M-theory. It appears to reconcile five competing versions of Superstring theory and introduces a sixth component called "eleven dimensional quantum gravity." This proposes a world with ten dimensions of space combined with a single dimension of time. If just trying to imagine ten dimensions of space caused a feedback loop in your brain, I've made my point. The truth is always greater and more complicated than we can imagine. This is why we use symbols, metaphors, and allegory to try to give our brains a foothold when it comes to understanding concepts that lie totally outside of our experience.

What do ten dimensions of space look like? I can't imagine and neither can any other human. M-theory and string theory are based on mathematical equations, not observations. Even if you could see a ten-dimensional object (assuming that your brain could make heads or tails of it), what could you then do? Draw a picture of it in two-dimensions? Make a 3D model of it? You get the point. Like Peirce's four-sided triangle, there is no grasping what can't even be conceived.* To even consider something so far outside the parameters of our reality, we have to make concessions. It turns out the simple truth isn't so simple. We must accept that our best understanding, and the best one that anybody could have, is going to be approximate, incomplete, or imperfect.

As Kabbalah postulates that the highest truth of God can never be known, symbols and approximations are the only way the Divine can even be contemplated. Even this, Kabbalah explains is part of the design. Humans are meant to experience *their* world. However, so each person might seek ever higher Truth according to their ability, humans perceive in their world a reflection of the higher world.

---

* Perhaps in an eleven dimensional world, four-sided triangles make sense.

Einstein in the home of colleague Paul Ehrenfest in 1916, a year after he published his theory of General Relativity.

CHAPTER 6

Let There Be Light

Light is among humanity's oldest and most universal symbols. In Masonry, it's a symbol of Truth, and masons refer to the personal journey of self-improvement as a search, or quest, for further *light*. Light has long been recognized as the source of life and the sun that provided it was anciently revered and often deified. At the dawn of humanity, the bright, warm light of day was certainly preferable to the dark, cold danger of night. For a species like humans that relies so heavily on eyesight for both hunting and defense, the difference between survival and extinction was literally night and day. With the advent of agriculture this only became more so.

It's easy to understand why, along with accounts of order brought from chaos, the creation myths of many early cultures include stories of light overcoming darkness. The creation narrative in Genesis, seen in the last chapter, is an excellent example. After God creates Heaven and Earth, he gives it a look over and says, "Let there be light." An initial creative act produced heaven and earth, but the addition of light brought the cold, dark world to life. It was the necessary first step in bringing order to the unformed void. With light, we see and can discern the good from the bad. *God saw the light, that it was good, and divided the light from the darkness (Genesis 1:4).*

If the light of day symbolizes one thing, then the dark of night naturally represents its opposite. When light represents the truth, dark symbolizes ignorance. When light is a symbol of life then dark is one of death. This seems very obvious, but there is a more subtle point to be made. Darkness is negative. It, itself, is not an attribute. It represents an absence. That is to say, it does not describe the presence of any characteristic that can be eliminated to remove the darkness. Darkness lacks essence. This is also symbolic. Darkness is not something bad which needs to be removed. It's not a stain or a blemish. It is the natural state of things, and the condition of darkness is only changed by the addition of light. In our universe, light appears here and there, now and then. Everywhere else and at all other times, is darkness. When masons refer to the uninitiated as being "in darkness," that is only suggestive of their natural and as yet unimproved state.

Masonry's mission includes, at its center, the search for *light* and the lifelong process of overcoming and eliminating *darkness*. The capacity of light to reveal what is hidden in the dark, long ago made it a fitting symbol for knowledge and learning, the revelation of Truth. Religions far and wide embrace *light* as such a symbol. Obviously, compared to ancient times, the conversation about matters of truth includes a lot less religion and much more science. However, a modern scientific perspective doesn't diminish the value of light as a symbol of truth. In fact, the discoveries of science and the truth as we understand it now, add quite a lot.

The more we learned about light, the more mysterious it seemed. Before quantum mechanics, the physical world was largely understood to consist of matter and energy. Matter was thought to exist as particles and energy as waves. Particles seemed to take up space and have mass, and waves apparently did neither. It seemed particles and waves were discrete concepts. That is, something was definitely one or the other. Light, however, was different. It exhibits characteristics of *both* and can't be precisely classified as either. Light appeared to be, in this way, peculiar. As science advanced into the twentieth century, realizing another peculiarity of light led to a monumental shift in the way humans understand the physical world.

In everyday language, we describe the speed of light, or anything else—a car on a highway, a runner on a course—in terms of time and space. Rate of speed, by this understanding, is the distance a thing travels through space, in ratio to the time it takes to travel that distance. To put the information in a context we understand, we often fix one, either the distance or the time, and measure the other. Sometimes, for example, we fix the time, say one hour, and measure the distance, perhaps sixty miles, and compute the car traveled sixty miles per hour. Other times we'll fix the distance, a mile for example, and measure the time, six minutes, and say someone ran a six-minute mile. Knowing the distance traveled and the time elapsed, we can calculate and describe the rate of speed for any moving object.

But what about a radar gun? A traffic officer, waiting for speeding cars on the freeway, has no knowledge of the distance you've traveled nor how much time you've been at it. How do they determine the speed of a car as it goes past them? Distance over time is just one way to describe speed, or velocity. It's the way most of us find familiar and one that we naturally understand, however it's not the only one. A radar gun detects the speed of an object by a different measurement. It emits radio waves which bounce off a moving object and come back to the gun where the frequency of the returning wave is measured. Moving objects, encountering the radio waves, create differences in the returning frequencies which indicate the speed of the moving object.

Now, the reason a traffic officer even needs a radar gun in the first place, is because a car *can* exceed the legal speed limit. A car might cruise along at twenty-five miles per hour or zip by at eighty. The speed of a car is variable. We assume, however, that time and space are constant. That is, if I normally make the thirty-mile drive to work in sixty minutes, but one morning I make the same drive in only forty minutes, the reasonable assumption would be that my speed was different, i.e., I drove faster today than yesterday. It would be much less likely that anyone would conclude thirty miles today was not the same as thirty miles was yesterday, or an hour yesterday is only equivalent to forty minutes today. Time and space are constant and speed is variable. Except, it turns out, that's not really the case.

Light, as we commonly describe it, travels at a speed so unimaginably fast (roughly 186,000 miles per second) that a particle moving at that rate would travel around the earth seven and a half times in one second! The speed of light has been measurable, with relatively good accuracy, since the end of the nineteenth century. Within a few decades, with improved measurement techniques, certain unusual qualities of light were noticed to be true. Puzzling and counterintuitive was the apparent fact that, unlike the speed of a commuter's car, which may vary from one instant to another, the speed of light is constant. It doesn't accelerate and it doesn't change to conform to time and space.

What does that mean? Going back to the car as an example, imagine a couple changes to our hypothetical automobile. First, imagine the car has been outfitted with a strict governor giving it a maximum speed of sixty miles per hour. The car gets going and moves past a radar gun and it's confirmed: it's going sixty. Next imagine the highway is a giant moving platform like the moving walkways in many airports. Suppose the highway moves at forty miles per hour. The car, now moving past a second radar gun, and being additionally sped up by our imaginary roadway, is clocked going a hundred. Now imagine you project a light and measure the speed of its beam with a laser. The light would be traveling at roughly 670,616,629 miles per hour. However if you started your moving roadway and accelerated the spotlight, no matter how fast the platform moved, the speed of light would never exceed that value.

The reality is, strange as it seems but proven and confirmed repeatedly by scientists since Einstein, time and space are not constant, but the speed of light is. Time and space, which so largely define the physical world, are, in fact, relative. Countless experiments have proven that time and distance both produce different measurements depending on the velocity of the observer and that velocity can never surpass the speed of light. According to the Laws of Nature, light speed is the absolute speed limit for our universe. Nothing can exceed it. Of course, the relativity of time and space is not a simple idea. For most of us, such counterintuitive concepts are absolutely baffling and Einstein's Theory of Special Relativity won't be made graspable by the crude summary given here. It's brought up to suggest that light, as the standard to which our physical world of time and space is calibrated, in a very literal way, connects us to reality. Even in a rigidly scientific sense, light is an excellent symbol of truth.

Kabbalah adds to this symbolism unique ideas concerning creation. Creation is more than either the created world or the outburst by which it came to exist. The unknowable divinity, *Ein Sof*, reveals particular aspects of itself. *Light* issues from hidden recesses and pours through the *sephirot*. This light not only forms, enlivens, and sustains the world, but is the representative of the Great Architect, the ambassador introducing itself on behalf of the mysterious source of everything. Creation is simultaneously an act of forming the world and a divine self-introduction. Light is a symbol of the creation and the Creator and represents every sublime attribute by which divinity may be known.

Rule the Day

As the literal source of light everywhere on Earth, the sun is a universal symbol. The sun was directly worshipped by more than a few ancient peoples. It not only brought light and heat, it marked the days and years, and outlined the seasons. Importantly for humans, the changes brought about by the sun were useful because they were predictable. The order and predictability of the world was so long ago observed and is now, so perfectly explained, that people today can't help but take it for granted. However, try to imagine living in a world where you couldn't predict nightfall or winter. Animals instinctively react to the changes in the daylight and the weather in their surrounding environment, and they migrate, hibernate, and otherwise prepare for upcoming seasons. Theirs is a response to a change in season that has already happened, not an ability to predict the coming winter. In years where unseasonably warm weather causes fall to be late, animals can be unprepared for the winter. It was a great advantage for humans to know that despite an unusually warm autumn, they should still prepare for snow. This is an advantage that mankind was afforded by a predictable and orderly world.

Today, it's well known that the sun is a star and that the earth is a planet that orbits it.[27] Sun worship now more readily conjures the image of beachgoers on a summer afternoon than it does Druids in front of a stone altar at the winter solstice. However the sun is no less rich a symbol now than it was then. It's been reinterpreted within modern contexts and in line with updated sensibilities. The sun, because it

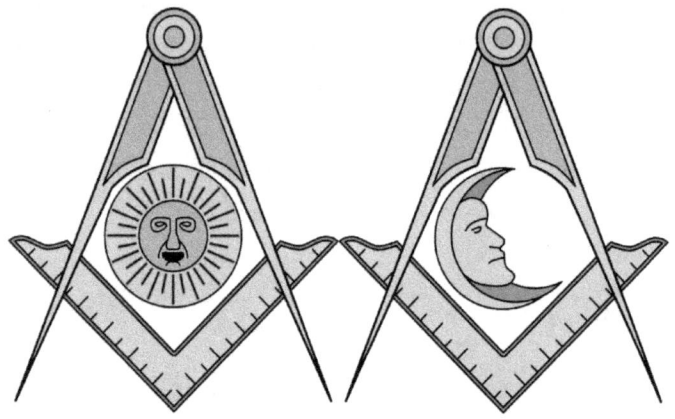

The sun and moon are common symbols in Freemasonry.

provides warmth, is today a symbol of warm feelings and is recognized as happy, friendly, or kind.

Masons maintain the sun as a symbol in several applications, each admitting different interpretations. More than simply a symbol of light, the sun was the *exclusive* source of light on earth. When it headed over the horizon, the light went with it. The sun was powerful. It decided whether the world was light or dark, warm or cold. Paraphrasing an expression from the Bible, the sun "*ruled the day.*" In a literal manner of speaking, the sun does "rule" the day. The sun's daily increase and decrease, roughly divided the daytime into morning, midday, and evening. In the sense in which "ruling" means "*drawing lines,*" the sun, indeed, "rules" the day. Of course, it's the Earth's rotation, not any actual "coming and going" of the sun, that "moves" the sun from east to west each day. But from our perspective, observed for millennia, the sun's position in the sky draws the lines between morning, afternoon, evening, and night.

Astrological relics, not concerning Zodiac signs or horoscopes, but referring metaphorically to the sun at different stages of the day, remain in masonic symbolism. This daily pattern of sunrise, mid-day, sunset, and night, was long ago related to stages of human life. The ancient Riddle of the Sphinx asked, "What walks on four feet in the morning, two feet at noon and three feet in the evening?" The answer, of course, is "man"—a human being—who crawls as a baby, walks as an adult, and, in old age, relies on a cane.

Without going deeper into possible interpretations of the ancient riddle, the relevant point is made. Morning, noon, and evening are very old symbols for youth, adulthood, and old age. The sun, in its daily march across the sky, portrays the span of life; the sunrise of birth to the twilight of the golden years. Light, by the gentle promise of daybreak, the blaze of midday, and the creeping at first, then sudden surrender into dusky sunset, was the symbol of the living spirit.

The sun may rule the day, but it doesn't do everything by itself. It has partners. The sun gives warmth and light to the Earth, and the Earth makes something with it. Plants, rooted in the Earth and fed by the sun, begin a cycle of life that includes all living things. Every form of life, human included, owes its existence to the same two sources: the Sun and the Earth. The Earth, symbolically impregnated with life, in many traditions, became a "Mother," while the Sun, as a stand in for divine providence, represented a heavenly "Father." The procreative act became a symbol of creation in general. This obvious association is the foundation of the *male/female* symbolism that appears, in many examples, throughout the ancient and medieval world. Physical existence is the product of a generative force applied to a receptive vessel. A "male" potential, something capable of being realized, meets a "female" potentiator, something able to realize it. A glowing example, if you will, of such symbolism, is the sun's symbolic relationship with its best known partner; the moon.

Govern the Night

The cycle of life illustrated by the daily progression from the youth of sunrise to the retirement of sunset, would inevitably arrive at the dark of night. When the sun adjourned in the evening, another heavenly body presided over the night; the moon. The moon, however, does not shine light of its own. By virtue of its position in the heavens, it reflects the light of the sun, in a limited, inconstant, and indirect way, to the Earth. This receptive capacity symbolically made the moon the *female* companion of the *male* sun. The symbolism of sun and moon is seen in Eastern and Western traditions alike. The moon, as an allegorical partner of the sun, is significantly developed in classical alchemical and Hermetic literature, where the sun and moon are associated with gold and silver. Alchemy maintained correspondences between the metals and the heavenly bodies known to the ancient and medieval world.[28] The sun and moon, according to their relatively large stature and more regular presence in the earth's sky, took preeminence, and were linked to the two precious metals.

Gold and silver, as valuable as they continue to be today, were, in ancient times, not simply currency but symbolic of royalty. Their perceived purity and incorruptibility made them appropriate symbols of majesty and the closeness to divinity which monarchs invariably assumed. If the provident sun made the nurturing and attendant earth a *mother*, then the distant and silvery moon, resplendent in the heavens, was made a *queen*, by the golden *king*. In Kabbalah, *the moon* symbolically refers to the sephirah *Malkhut*. Most often translated as *kingdom*, *malkhut* is probably better translated as "kingliness." It doesn't refer to the geographical territory or domain over which a monarch is sovereign, but rather to the essential quality of being a king. The idea encompasses the regality, royalty, and majesty of a monarch. The Hebrew root word prefers no gender so the word is just as well understood as "queenliness" or "sovereignliness." *Malkhut*, as the *moon* reflects the light of the *sun* to the world below.*

* The "sun" is Tif'eret.

Referring back to Genesis, the sun rules the day and the moon governs the night.

Usually playing second fiddle to the sun, the moon is, itself, a valuable symbol. The reflected light of the moon illuminates the dark. This point deserves more attention than it usually receives. As said earlier, knowledge and the various pursuits of it are, today, very specialized. Science and philosophy are vast realms, and the accumulated amount of information is enormous. A contemporary human, living in developed society, is navigating a world in which practically every other step is taken in the dark. We rely on communication, currency, and countless other systems, the inner workings of which most can't, or don't, even fathom. In the many instances where we find ourselves "in the dark" so to speak, involved in some matter about which we know little or nothing, we rely on the reflected light of others. The sun rules the day by the direct influence of its own light, however, the moon presides over the night by properly reflecting the light of others.

Not only is the light of the moon indirect, it waxes and wanes. Sometimes the full moon is radiant and complete and other times, the moon is a paltry sliver, and the light barely shows the ground ahead. So it is that when one doesn't know a great deal to start with, and is totally reliant on the input of others, seeking the truth is especially fraught with both difficulty and danger. Searches begun in "darkness," that is, from a place of total ignorance, can be frustrating, disorienting, and, at times, completely misleading. This is symbolic of the quest for light in its earliest stages, when it's not always clear or possible to tell where next to turn. We rely on others, at first to reflect light while we are in darkness, but soon to lead us into the light ourselves.

The waxing and waning of the reflected light of the moon is another symbol of human experience. In some ways, our entire existence occurs "in the dark" and everything we see, feel, and know is only a reflection. Prior to modern understandings of anatomy, people believed that vision resulted from a process called extramission, where "beams" believed to be emitted from the eyes were thought to make objects visible. We know now light doesn't come out of the eyes but that vision results from reflected light instead entering our eyes. The point is, *everything* we see is reflected light. Rather than seeing the *moon* and its reflected light as poor and diminished, it is appropriate to see the moon also as a symbol of providence. The gift of light, even in the night. Sometimes, just enough to overcome the darkness. Never assuming the full brilliance of the sun. The inconsistent and indeliberate moon, with its, imperfect but attendant light, relays the glimmer of hope and a reassurance that the full light of the sun is waiting just beyond the dawn.

With this general overview complete, it is time to look at Kabbalah's crown jewel, the *Zohar*. The teachings of Kabbalah are as wonderful as they are strange. The symbols of Masonry are a treasure, though, in many cases, one waiting to be unearthed. Speculative Masonry's original mission to reconcile the symbols of popular traditions with the ideas of "natural philosophy" aka science, has long lain about, practically discontinued. This was once the mission of Kabbalah, who acquitted itself so handsomely in that duty that very few—not the greater portion of Judaism and much less the world at large—are aware of the great work that was done. However, great work *was* done. In that work is found an example by which Masonry, after more than a forty year sojourn in the wilderness, can lead itself into the promised land.

"'Lord, if Pharaoh says to me, Who are you, how am I to answer him?' Then the Lord said: 'Then say I am that I am has sent you.' That means, he who is immutable in himself, he has sent me."

Meister Eckhart, On Detachment

PART II

I am what I am

The wise will shine like the radiance of heaven

The questions of religion, ethics, science, and philosophy are all, at their essence, questions about existence. Why do we exist? How did we come to exist? How should we continue to exist? What else exists with us? What does it mean to exist at all? The first of the three points upon which we all agree, is simply, the world exists. This simple statement, however, implicitly comes with all these questions. Existence is the great first mystery. Perhaps it's not surprising that the simple idea that God is synonymous with existence is among the highest concepts of deity. God is not *a being*, God is *Being*.

This idea appears in the Bible story where Moses miraculously delivers the people of Israel through the Red Sea. As the account is written, before accepting this mission, Moses suffers a crisis of confidence. Not sure how he'll be received, Moses asks God who he should say is the one who sent him. "*They say to me 'what is His name?' What shall I tell them?*" *(Exodus 3:13)* God's response is "*Ehyeh asher ehyeh, I am that which I am . . . say . . . 'I am has sent me to you'*" (ibid. 14). *Ehyeh*, given here to Moses as a name of God—the only instance where it's used as such—is as common a word as there is in the Bible. It literally means 'to be' and appears in the biblical text thousands of times translated as "*let there be*," "*there was*," "*there became*," "*it shall be*," etc. The better-known, traditional *name* of God, YHVH (יהוה), is formed from a similar root, also implying *becoming.*[*] The God of the Bible is very literally connected to the idea of existence.

With that in mind, here is the *Zohar*, at least a few slices of it. Be warned. If this is your first approach, the passages you are about to read are likely to make very little sense. Don't be discouraged. As the symbols are explained, more meaning will become clear. It's almost always the case in Kabbalah, that there is more in these passages than will be explained. To include everything would be impossible. I've tried, with all the examples that follow, to make those points which are relevant to Masonry and to the ideas of this book.

Title page from the first print edition of the *Zohar*, the 1558 Mantua edition.

Zohar 3:65a, Parashat Aharei Mot

"He said to him, 'If it please my father, I have heard about what is written: (*Ehyeh asher ehyeh*), *I am that I am* (Exodus 3:14), and I do not fathom it.'

He replied, "El'azar, my son, the Companions have already established this, and now all is bound in one entity. Mystery of the matter is as follows: אהיה (*Ehyeh*), *I am*—totality of all, for when paths are concealed, not diverging, included in one place, then it is called *Ehyeh*, totality of all, hidden and not revealed. Once a beginning emerges and that river is impregnated, to channel all, then it is called אשר אהיה (*asher ehyeh*), *that I am*, meaning: 'Until here *I am*; *I am* ready to convey and give birth to all.'"

For readers new to the *Zohar*, this passage provides an example of what might be expected. The text is often presented as a conversation

---

[*] *Ehyeh* (אהיה) is formed from the root היה (HYH) which means to be or become. YHVH (יהוה) is formed from the root הוה (HVH) which similarly means being or becoming but also carries a sense of doing.

between rabbis. Rabbi El'azar is here asking his father, Rabbi Shim'on, to explain a bible verse. The younger rabbi asks about the episode where God appears to Moses in the burning bush. The explanation he receives is, typical of Kabbalah, enigmatic. Moses, asking the name by which he should identify God, is told, *"Ehyeh asher ehyeh, (I am that which I am) . . . say to them, Ehyeh sent you."* The kabbalists, interpreting the text literally, take *Ehyeh* to be a particularly special name for God, one which is only revealed here to Moses.

The Hebrew word Ehyeh (אהיה), translated as *I am* in this example, may also be understood in the future tense; *I will be*. So the verse can be read *"I will be what I will be," "I am what I will be"* or *"I will be what I am."* Any of those translations is possible and each of these meanings is implied in the Hebrew text. Rabbi Shim'on elaborates on the expression piece by piece. The first *ehyeh* of the phrase, he explains strangely. *"Ehyeh—totality of all, for when paths are concealed, not diverging, included in one place, then it is called Ehyeh, totality of all, hidden and not revealed."* The rest of the explanation is equally unclear. He tells his son that once a *"beginning emerged"* and a *"river was impregnated"* then that which had previously been known as *ehyeh, I am*, would thereafter be known as *asher ehyeh, that I am.*

If that clarified things for you, your knowledge of Kabbalah is better than most. For the rest, here's an explanation. Throughout this book, existence has been considered in two dimensions, potential and actual. The first *ehyeh*, taken by itself and removed from context, refers to *being* in general. *"Ehyeh—totality of all, . . . not diverging . . . then it is called . . . hidden and not revealed."* Shim'on is referring to everything in pre-existent potential—*"totality of all, hidden and not revealed." I am*. Existence in general—*"not diverging"*—without the separateness of particular existence. The potential for *everything* without the realization of anything. I am not *this* or *that*, I am not a specific *thing*, I simply *am*. All as a singularity.

The word *asher, that which*, is particular. So the second part, *asher ehyeh*, includes context and refers to a specific being; *that which I am.*

The phrase, explained this way, may be understood as "*I am (in general) therefore I shall be (specifically)*." The relationship is then made explicit. Shim'on explains the meaning is "*I am ready to convey and give birth to all.*"

This is a glimpse into the bewildering world of the *Zohar*. The language is a layered pile of symbolism, nearly all of which is centered on the *sephirot*. Very little is meant to be understood as it appears, and a good amount of explanation is needed to interpret its passages meaningfully. In the *Zohar*, the stories and characters of the Bible, are all symbolic allusions to the *sephirot*. In the end, there is only one story in Kabbalah, that of existence. That shouldn't be understood to mean, however, that the story is simple. In fact, nothing could possibly be more complex. The world must not only be created, which is no small process in itself, it must be maintained. All of this concerns the *sephirot*.

Though it wasn't explained, even the symbolism in this example refers to the *sephirot*. Several kabbalistic traditions are quietly alluded to in the passage. An important one relates different names of God to the *sephirot*. According to this, the mysterious name *Ehyeh* refers to the first sephirah, *Keter*, the divine Will. Two other traditions, about to be explained, refer to *Hokhmah* and *Binah*. Without a small understanding of these, much will be irrecoverable from the jumble of symbolic language.

Before the "Big Bang" there was, presumably, nothing; no matter, no space, no time. *Nothing*. Hence the crucial question for philosophers, scientists, and theologians to this day. How did everything come from nothing? The concept of *creatio ex nihilo*, creation out of nothing, is another, which, at its roots, seems contrary to experience. Things don't appear "out of thin air." It goes against a fundamental law of the universe. *The total amount of matter in a closed system remains constant over time.** In simple terms, matter can neither be created nor destroyed, it can only change from one form to another. So where did everything come from? We're still trying to figure that out.

All creation accounts are essentially similar. An initial state of *non-being* arrives at *being*. It's the details of what happens in between that

---

* The Law of Conservation of Matter.

vary across traditions. Despite great advances in science, the speculation continues, even today. Existence and its origin are a great mystery. What can be said with relative certainty is the world *is*, but it used to *not be*. Perhaps this is not much of a revelation. Many ancient thinkers already believed this. By the Middle Ages, however, a broader sophistication in thinking prompted a corresponding need for better explanations. Starting with Saadia Gaon (882–942 CE) and reaching a head with Maimonides' *Guide for the Perplexed*, Jewish philosophy increasingly called their religious tradition into question.

To the average religionist, the direct indictments of tradition were more important than abstract questions about being and non-being. The specific question of how God can be simultaneously transcendent and immanent was particularly difficult. If God was, as the philosophers insisted, beyond human contact, then how was He also present among the people, as tradition taught? This is a simple example of the increasing incongruity between traditional ways of thinking and new ideas. The following passage from the *Zohar*, includes, among much else, a direct response to the challenges of rationalist philosophers.

Zohar Hadash, Bereshit, 17b, Midrash ha-Neʾelam

Rabbi Tanhum opened, "*Thus says God, YHVH, who creates the heavens and stretches them out* . . . (Isaiah 42:5). When the blessed Holy One created His world, He created them from nothing, bringing them into actuality, imbuing them with substance. Wherever you find בורא (*bore*), *create*, it refers to something He created from nothing and brought into actuality."

Rav Hisda asked "But were the heavens really created from nothing? Weren't they created from the light above?"
Rabbi Tanhum replied, "It is so—the matter of the heavens came from nothing, but their form from an entity of substance; similarly with the human being.

"Concerning the heavens you will find (*beriʾah*), *creating*, and afterward (*asiyyah*), *making. Creating—who creates the heavens* (Isaiah 42:5); in other words, from nothing. *Making—who makes the heavens* (Psalms 136:5), from an entity of substance, from the light above."

Rabbi Tanhum also said, "*Asiyyah, making*, refers to the enhancement of something in terms of its size and stature—compared to
how it was before—as is said: David (*va-ya'as*), *enhanced*, his name
(2 Samuel 8:13)."

To both kabbalists and rationalists, *creation from nothing* was an
important concept. The opposite notion, *creatio ex materia, creation from
matter*, implied a great deal that is difficult to sustain religiously. Any
idea that matter was eternal and coexisted with God was troublesome.
In this example, Rabbi Tanhum, explains a verse from Isaiah, "*Thus says
God, YHVH, who creates the heavens and stretches them out . . .*" The rabbi
teaches that when the Hebrew verb, *bore*, (*create*) is used in scripture,
it implies creation from nothing. What then follows is an example of
Kabbalah coming to the defense of tradition. Rav Hisda, one of Tanhum's
companions, questions this teaching. Hisda refers to a midrash in which
Rabbi Eliezar the Great, a legendary figure and occasional star of the
Zohar, taught that the heavens were made, not from *nothing*, but from
light. This teaching was the subject of direct and heavy criticism from
Maimonides.[29] Hisda therefore asks if the heavens were created from
nothing or, as Eliezar taught, from *light*.

Despite initially agreeing with the philosopher on the specific point
of creation from nothing, Tanhum comes to the defense of Eliezar's
assailed legacy. Tanhum confirms the heavens were, as he said himself,
created from nothing, but says Eliezar was also correct. He invokes the
kabbalistic idea that the word *creation* (Hebrew *beri'ah*) refers to just
one step of the generative process. It's followed by *making* (*asiyyah*),
which is a separate stage of the process. Tanhum explains this is clearly
indicated in the Bible, where it's written in one place "*who creates the
heavens*" (*Isaiah 42:5*) and in another "*who makes the heavens*" (*Psalms
136:5*). The difference between the two stages is further expressed, when
it's said *making* refers to the enhancing of *size and stature*.

Earlier, I said things don't "appear out of thin air." However, that's not entirely true. Perhaps the one earthly semblance of *something* brought from *nothing* is a human being's own creative power. Among mankind's great gifts, is the ability to imagine what doesn't exist and intentionally produce something actual from potential. Kabbalists were among those who imagined the origin of the universe from nothing could have occurred according to a similar creative process within divinity. Human creativity became both evidence and a symbol of divine creativity. The unknown force behind creation was illustrated as a human artisan, or builder, creating a physical object from an idea. Even to the artist who conceives it, the design of a work often seems to come from nowhere other than their own will and an unnameable *higher source* of inspiration. The *Creator*, in whatever form it was imagined, was depicted as bringing everything into *being* from the unimaginable condition of *non-being*, according only to its own mysterious will; a first cause.

The *sephirot*, and the symbolic worlds they spawned, metaphorically fill the distance between the inconceivable "Cause above all Causes" and the omnipresence of God "in His Tabernacle." Between the distant concept of *Ein Sof*, and the immediacy of the Shekinah who cares and provides for the people, span the *sephirot*. Ten heavenly units which map the gradual emergence of *being* from *non-being*, and maintain the unity of the ideal world of heaven and God who occupies it, and the real world of earth and God who dwells here among us. The *sephirot* provide a conceptual "ladder" by which to approach and imagine, in some useful way, the unimaginable. As written in the *Shomer Emunim*:

Creation depicted as the work of a builder or architect.

    ... we do not have the ability

to involve ourselves with what happened before the emanation of the 10 Sephirot and cannot imagine any form or likeness of it at all, God forbid. However, so that it can be related to in human terms, we must use an analogy and a wise person will understand on his own that there is no existence of any [such] form at all there, God forbid. However it is [only] from the [level of the] 10 Sephirot and below that it is possible to [meaningfully] speak in terms of a parable and analogy.

The thought of pre-existence is impossible to conceive. For this reason, the language of the *Zohar* always refers symbolically to the *sephirot*. In the previous example, reference is made to the first *sephirah*, *Keter*, by the nickname *Ayin*, nothing. With this being the first emanation and the source of all subsequent creation, Kabbalah emblematically accomplishes creation from nothing. *Keter* also symbolizes the divine *Will*. Kabbalah, with its multi-layered symbolism, reflects the mysterious and impenetrable nature of pre-existence. The *nothing* from which the world was created is simply another reference to that portion of the unknowable we symbolize as divine will.

Pilgrims visit the tomb of second century sage, Rabbi Shimon Bar Yochai, pseudepigraphic author of the *Zohar*.

The Beginning is Wisdom

The title of this book comes from a fundamental tenet of Kabbalah: the Beginning *is* Wisdom. The phrase may sound as though it's leaving out an important detail; the beginning of what? However, nothing is missing. The idea is fully expressed as intended, and comes from a reading of Psalms 111:10.[30] Typically translated in English as "the beginning of wisdom", the closing words of the verse are, in Hebrew, just two: ראשית (*reshit*), *beginning*, and חכמה (*hokhmah*), *wisdom*. The English preposition "of" is inferred by translators from the surrounding context. Kabbalists, however, as a practice, will take a phrase like this entirely out of context, and interpret it hyper-literally. The two words, *reshit hokhmah*, were instead read as "reshit *is* hokhmah"—*the Beginning is Wisdom*. This approach, interpreting expressions outside of the narrative context, gives Kabbalah a unique—sometimes bizarre—and practically unlimited flexibility.

Kabbalistically, the Beginning *is* Wisdom in the same way that two plus two *is* four. That is, the Beginning *equals* Wisdom. One word is a symbol of the other word. As symbols of one another, every piece of scripture including either word is reinterpretable. Replacing one word with the other, the opening verse of the Bible goes from "*In the Beginning*" to "*In Wisdom,*" and immediately suggests a host of new meanings. "*The beginning*" doesn't signify a remote point in time, but refers to the *sephirah Hokhmah*, the site of divine Thought, or abstract Wisdom. Therefore in Kabbalah, the verse is understood, 'In *Wisdom*, God created the Heavens and the Earth.'[31]

In Wisdom God created. . .

Kabbalah's symbolic *Beginning*, is a fitting place to initiate a look at the *Zohar*. In this undeniably poetic expression—*the Beginning is Wisdom*—is more than one excellent example of Kabbalah's unique approach. Suggestive as the phrase plainly is, there is substance to the artful wordplay. Speaking, not of *when* God created the world but *how*, changes the Bible from history to philosophy. With this one shift, the Bible stops being an inconsistent and unreliable history book, and becomes a description, explanation, and, ultimately, celebration of the world and mankind's relationship to it.

The *sephirot* are unusually rich symbols. The many names by which they are identified, appear commonly throughout scripture. For kabbalists, any occurrence refers to more than the word's plain meaning. Each moniker identifies a *sephirah* and, more generally, refers to the abstract quality it expresses. As one of the sephirot, *Hokhmah* is more than just a Hebrew word for *wisdom* or *thought*. It represents all the concepts associated with the *sephirah* by each of its different names. The affiliation of otherwise unrelated concepts with the same *sephirah*, made them symbols of each other. In the end, the word *hokhmah* is a symbol for the idea of Wisdom, and the idea of Wisdom is a symbol of the *sephirah* called *Hokhmah*—and everything else that *sephirah* represents. If this isn't entirely clear yet, it will become more so as further examples are explained. In the meantime, remember the *sephirot* are more than simply the names of divine attributes. The Beginning is Wisdom, and also Wisdom is the Beginning.

Before One, what do you count?

That *Hokhmah* is "*the beginning*" seems to contradict the fact that *Keter* is actually the first *sephirah*. The kabbalists however, are insistent; *Hokhmah* is the beginning. This emphasizes the secret nature of *Keter*, the divine Will, subtly revealed but essentially unknowable, and called *ayin*, nothing. Symbolically the *nothingness* of *Keter*, is best expressed by the number zero. This makes *Hokhmah* number one. As is written in the *Sefer Yetzirah*, "Before One, what do you count?" In the *Zohar*, *Keter* is usually referred to only indirectly. This intentional understatement, seen in the next example, is another kabbalistic method for symbolizing the subtlety and ineffability of the very highest conceptions of divinity.

In Kabbalah, the initial act of creation is not physical but intellectual. In "wisdom" God created the Heavens and the Earth (*Genesis 1:1*), provides a unique view of the Biblical account. According to this perspective, the world was first *created* in divine *thought* or *wisdom*, the *sephirah Hokhmah*. Before anything was formed, all existed as a complete thought. There was a *plan* for creation. The world was brought into being according to this blueprint. The following excerpt from the *Zohar* was selected partially because, in keeping with masonic symbolism, it depicts Deity as an *architect*. Heaven and Earth are created symbolically *in Wisdom*. Creation, again is a process of realizing potential.

The word *esoteric*, associated frequently with both Kabbalah and Freemasonry, is a sophisticated way of saying "if you know, you know." Its esoteric nature makes Kabbalah difficult or impossible for those who "don't know" to interpret. The kabbalists were, after all, rabbis. Their writings often refer, sometimes openly, sometimes indirectly, to legends and traditions familiar to educated Jewish readers, but likely not to others. The selection that follows alludes to two such traditions relevant to this book. One tradition, of obvious note to freemasons, symbolizes divinity as an *architect*.[32] Another, says that the *Torah, the Law*, existed before Creation and is the blueprint for the universe. These two ideas—God is the architect of heaven and earth, and *the Law* is the blueprint—provide the subtext of the passage.

Zohar I, 90a, Sitrei Torah

[Rabbi Eleazar] opened, saying: "*The* LORD *is in His holy palace, be silent before Him, all the earth!*" (Habakkuk 2:20). When the blessed Holy One wanted to create the world, He gazed into Thought—the mystery of the Torah—and He drew sketches.[33] But it could not endure until He created *Teshuvah*, repentance—inner, supernal palace, hidden mystery. Letters sketched and formed[34] there in their engravings. After this creation, He gazed from this Palace, sketching designs[35] of the entire world. This is as is written: Silent before Him, all the earth! (ibid.).

Eleazar, another of the quasi-legendary rabbis who star in the *Zohar*, opens with a verse from Habakkuk.* What follows is unclear. He provides an explanation which seems irrelevant to the verse. The Great Architect is described as drawing the plans for creation. To begin, God *"gazed into Thought"* and designs were drawn there. Those plans, however, *"could not endure"* until *"He created repentance."* Once this happens, the initial blueprint takes form and further designs become possible. This bizarre presentation is intended to explain the last phrase of the verse, *silent before Him, all the earth,* but it's difficult to see how it even makes sense. Oddities like this are common in the *Zohar* and can't be understood at face value.

If you are familiar with Kabbalah, you may immediately recognize some symbols in the text. Two words, *Thought* and *Repentance,* refer to the *sephirot Hokhmah* and *Binah,* respectively. The reference to *Hokhmah* is direct, but *Binah* is referred to using a kabbalistic alias, *teshuvah, repentance.*† The plans etched in *Hokhmah* could not "endure" until the next *sephirah, Binah,* called *repentance,* came into existence. Eleazar suggests that the verse should therefore be read, not in the imperative *"be* silent before Him," but descriptively as *"it was* silent before Him, all the earth!"‡ That is, *all the earth* existed *silently* in full potential in the divine Thought. Until Understanding appeared, Wisdom stood unable to be expressed. So Eleazer explains, it was *"silent* before Him." The passage continues.

Zohar I, 90a, Sitrei Torah (cont.)

He wanted to create the heavens. What did He do? Gazed into the primordial light, and clothed Himself in it, and created the heavens. This is as is written: *"Puts on light like a garment"* (Psalms 104:2), and then *"spreading the heavens like a curtain"* (ibid.).

---

* The *Zohar* largely takes the form of midrash, portraying the sayings and discussions of historically important rabbis. The rabbis of the *Zohar* often suggest historical persons however many of the identifying details are inconsistent or historically inaccurate.

† This is according to an early, established tradition of *Binah* being identified with repentance.

‡ The Hebrew word חס (*has*) simply means silent. The imperative form, "be silent," explicit in English, is implied in Hebrew, and the verse can correctly be understood either way.

"He gazed, to fashion the lower world. He produced another palace and entered into it. From there He gazed, sketching[36] before Him all the worlds below, creating them. This is as is written: "*The LORD is in His holy palace. Be silent before Him, all the earth!*" הס (*has*), *be silent*—inscribed before Him, sixty-five points of the entire world—numerical value of הס (*has*).

Eleazar continues, providing a second, perhaps stranger interpretation. God creates *the Heavens* and another *palace* is formed. For the studious, it's worth noting the Hebrew word *hekhal* (היכל), here translated as "palace," is the same word later translated as King Solomon's "temple." The phrase "*the Heavens*" is a common kabbalistic symbol for *Tif'eret*, and in a more general way, of the six lower *sephirot* apart from *Malkhut*.[37] Divinity enters this *palace* and only the lower world remains "*before Him*" to be designed.

In his second explanation, Eleazar says the Hebrew word הס (*has*), *silent*, refers to the "sixty-five points of all the world" according to its numerical value. This relies on a tradition called *Gematria*, a type of numerology using the Hebrew alphabet. Hebrew, like other ancient languages, doesn't have separate characters for numbers. Each letter of the alphabet does "double duty." In addition to its phonetic value, each character also has a numerical value. By extension, every word also has a numerical value, calculated by the sum of its letters.[38] The numerical value of word הס (*has*), "silent," is sixty-five, but Eleazar leaves the significance of this unexplained.

As promised, the *Zohar* is puzzling. It routinely gives different, perhaps, entirely unrelated interpretations of the same verse. As kabbalists are quick to explain, the truth appears differently relative to the distinct perspective of the observer. Eleazar's first explanation is applicable when Creation is in its earliest stages. All was then "silent," like a thought, maintained and pondered privately, awaiting expression. When the process advances, a second explanation is required. The word, *silent*, is interpreted as a number, *sixty-five*. This is also the numerical value of אדני (*adonai*), "my Lord," a common name for God and another alias for

Malkhut, the *Shekinah*.[39] A recurring theme of the *Zohar* is the divine romance of the *Shekinah*, courted by, betrothed to, and the beloved of *Tif'eret*. In this relationship with *Tif'eret*, who is called *heaven*, *Malkhut* is correspondingly called *earth*. So, Eleazar explains, "*silent*" is a symbol for *Malkhut*—"*all the earth*"—and it's that sephirah which is before Him.

Kabbalah is rarely straightforward. The original verse, *silent* before Him, read instead as *sixty-five* before Him, equates numerically to *Adonai* before Him, which is a nickname for *Malkhut* before Him. What remained "*before Him*,"— what was left to create—was *Malkhut*, aka *all the earth*. The layers of symbolism are dense. A number refers to a word, which is a nickname for an idea that symbolizes another idea and so on. It's easy to get lost or confused. Despite the intricate symbolism, there is something basic to consider.

The entire scene presents the image of the Creator in the role of *Master Builder*. Masons no doubt see the *Great Architect of the Universe*. The Supreme Builder is not laying stones but drawing designs. These designs symbolize the Law of the Universe, by which the world first becomes possible and eventually becomes real. This symbolism of *the Law* invites consideration of the magnificence of nature and the laws by which the countless parts of an unfathomably complex universe, are so nicely fit together.

The story Eleazar tells is one of potential and potentiator. *Hokhmah* waits to be realized until *Binah* makes it real. In Kabbalah, Wisdom is abstract potential made real by Understanding. Think of sound as an example. The earth is alive with sound, or more correctly, with sound waves. However, for as many sound waves as a person hears, there are many, many more that they don't hear. Frequencies either too high or too low, are imperceptible to humans. Dogs and cats hear much higher frequencies, and so dog whistles are loud and clear to them, but make no sound to humans. The wave needs to be heard or it doesn't make a sound. In the same way, *wisdom* must be *understood* to become practical knowledge.

This idea of realizing potential, is key to the masonic ideal of self-improvement. First imagine what you might be, then do your best to become it. There is more, in this and in all the passages presented here, that could be explained. Some you will understand as you read further. Practical considerations however, and some observance of the proper spirit of Kabbalah, require some things to be left for the curious to discover on their own.

Legendary philosopher Lao Tzu is depicted presenting his most famous work, the *Tao Te Ching*.

The Heavens and the Earth

In the beginning, so we read, *God created the Heavens and the Earth*. In earlier chapters, the symbols of *Heaven* and *Earth* were associated with a large number of concepts. What all of those examples—*ideal* and *real*, *potential* and *actual*, *soul* and *body*, *thought* and *word*—have in common, is that *Heaven*, in each case, represents something conceptual, and *Earth*, correspondingly, represents the physical image or manifestation of that idea. The Square and Compass, symbolizing the *Earth* and the *Heavens*, are, like the symbols of Kabbalah, compounded with meaning. Since the objects they symbolize, *Heaven* and *Earth*, are symbols themselves, the Compass and Square additionally represent everything that those symbols represent.

As above, so below

The idea that our physical world should reflect a perfect "world above" is not unique to Kabbalah or Freemasonry. The same concept is found in a host of traditions; those of Lao Tzu, Hermes Trismegistus, and Jesus of Nazareth, to name only three.* *As above, so below*, famously goes the Hermetic maxim, taken from a piece of literature known as the *Emerald Tablet*. Produced in the late ancient Egypt of the Ptolemies (c. 305–30 BCE), a body of magical, alchemical, and theosophical writings were attributed to a legendary Greco-Egyptian character called Hermes Trismegistus. Rediscovered to Europeans in the fifteenth century, the *Corpus Hermeticum*, as the collection came to be known, has enamored philosophers and theologians ever since. Even today, these writings, with their long exerted influence on alchemy and the occult, retain a particular interest for many freemasons. Several versions of the *Emerald Tablet* have surfaced through the years, and though it's likely impossible

---

* "The Earth models itself after Heaven," Tao Te Ching; "As above, so below," Emerald Tablet; "On Earth as in Heaven," Lord's Prayer.

to recover an "original" text, all existing sources agree on the primary point. What is *above* is mysteriously reflected in that which is *below*.

The *Zohar* presents this concept in its own inimitable way. In Kabbalah, the physical world is patterned after the *world above*. But our *world below* more than simply resembles or mirrors the higher world; each is intrinsic to the other's existence. Like a thought has no form without a word to express it, and a word has no substance except the thought it expresses, above and below are inextricably, existentially bound. Twentieth century scholar Isaiah Tishby explains the relationship between the *sephirot* and Creation itself:

> [It is] one of the basic principles of kabbalistic teaching, which recurs time and time again in the *Zohar*: the worlds, with all the beings they contain, and especially man, are constructed on the pattern of the *sefirot*, 'according to the form that is above.' The sefirot are the divine master-copy of nondivine existence, both in general and in particular. (Tishby, 273)

The *above/below* symbolism, in general, depicts existence as actualized potential, the unity of two potencies. Potential above, that which can be realized, with actualization below, that which can realize it. Using this illustration, the next passage expresses the sameness and the connectedness of *above* and *below*, the unity of *Heaven* and *Earth*, and, for freemasons, the union of the *Square* and *Compass*.

Zohar II, 20a, Midrash ha Ne'elam

> Rabbi Shimon said, "Woe to the creatures who are unaware, who do not know! When it arose in Thought before the blessed Holy One to create His world, all worlds arose in a single thought; and with this thought they were all created, as is written: "*With wisdom have You made them all*" (Psalms 104:24). With this thought—which is Wisdom—this world and the world above were created.

> He stretched out His right hand and created the world above; He stretched out his left hand and created this world, as is written: "*My hand founded the earth, and My right hand spread out heaven. I summon them—they stand together.*" (Isaiah 48:13)—all of them

were created in a single moment, a single instant.

He fashioned this world corresponding to the world above; all that is above has its counterpart below; and all that is below has its counterpart in the sea—all is one.

Some of the symbolism may be familiar from earlier examples. *Hokhmah*, called again by the alias *Thought*, is once more, the *Beginning* of the creative process. The *above/below* symbolism is portrayed both as *heaven* and *earth* and as the *world above* and the *world below*. The symbolism of *right* and *left* exists in close proximity to the symbolism of *above* and *below*, and, in some cases, the two overlap. A brief mention of *left* and *right* symbolism is made without elaboration. Finally, living up to the *Zohar*'s reputation for being arcane, the selection concludes with a strange sign-off, "all that is above has its counterpart below; and all that is below has its counterpart *in the sea*—all is one."

The expositor in this selection, is none other than Rabbi Shim'on ben Yohai, first century sage and pseudepigraphic author of the *Zohar*. The venerable rabbi begins his presentation with woe to those who "do not know." This is a standard kabbalistic device referring to the uninitiated, i.e., those who "*do not know*" the kabbalistic wisdom. What they don't know, he explains, is that "all worlds" exist the moment they are conceived in the divine mind. Shim'on teaches "all worlds arose in a single thought; and with this thought they were all created." He invokes for his explanation Psalms 104:24 "*in wisdom you created them all*" and Isaiah 48:13 "*I summon them, they stand together.*" Again, creativity is an *intellectual* act and existence begins with the initial thought or idea.

The biblical story of creation is traditionally understood to refer to the beginning of the physical universe. However, in Kabbalah, this is not necessarily the case. The creation story begins with the divine *intention* for the world. As already explained, the process of generation has multiple steps. For kabbalists, *creating* is not the same as *making*.

Above and *below*, *heaven* and *earth*, only exist together. They can be thought about discreetly, like the "heads" and "tails" of a coin, but they can't exist separately. There is no *one-sided coin*. According to the *Zohar*, this is the meaning of the verse, *I summon them—they stand together* (*Isaiah 48:13*). The primary message is the unity underlying all of existence (*they stand together*).

Again, this example includes references which are mostly unknown to outsiders. To emphasize the *sameness* of "the world above" and "the world below," Shim'on includes a reference to *the sea*, "...*all that is above has its counterpart below; and all that is below has its counterpart in the sea.*" No explanation follows. He alludes to a Talmudic legend that states "everything existing on land, exists in the sea."[40] In the *Zohar*, *the sea* is a well attested symbol. *Malkhut*, the last *sephirah*, who receives the abundance of all the others, is the *sea* into which all rivers pour. The rabbi is simply returning to his initial point, the unity of creation. Kabbalists suggest everything God intended for the world is reflected in the structure of heaven and the divine presence on earth.

The sage capstones his lesson with the kabbalistic refrain; *all is one*. Not all *are* one—but all *is* one. These classifications—*above, below, heaven, earth, the sea*—are not to be thought of as separate parts assembled to form a greater whole, but only as distinct perspectives of one seamless reality. Difference or separateness is an illusion and only a matter of the point of view. Reality compares to a ray of light shining down through a prism to what's below. Above the prism, the light is undifferentiated and imperceptible. However looking below the prism, the light is visibly arrayed in separate colors. The essence of the light is the same, it is the perspective which, in either case, is different. The *world above* and the *world below* are simply different expressions of *the Law*. All is one.

Creation, Formation, and other Worlds

Though creation happens in the first verse of the Bible, in the second verse, the Earth is still *unformed*. It's been explained that multiple steps are involved in bringing the whole world—or anything else—into existence. The several distinct steps understood by kabbalists are taken from a verse in the book of Isaiah. *Creation* is just the beginning. Along with *creation*, we've also seen there is *making*. In the next example, another stage is introduced to the process, *formation*. *Creating* is intellectual, *making* is physical, and *formation* occurs between those two. The world and everything in it were *created* with thought. Separate processes gave it all *form* and prepared it to be *made*.

Taking the verse "*I created him for My Glory. I formed him; indeed, I have made him.*" (*Isaiah 43:7*), the kabbalists teach that the three similar Hebrew words—*created*, *formed*, and *made*—are not redundant. Each word specifically refers to different processes. *Beri'ah* (creation), *yetzirah* (formation), and *asiyyah* (making), are distinct actions, each one describing a discrete stage of generation. This explains why after creation, the Earth was still not formed. The subsequent process of *formation* had not yet taken place. Formation is the step where generalized or abstract ideas take shape and become intelligible. If creation is a level of *thought*, formation is a level of *speech* or *language*. It's where existence is prepared for the transition from ideal to real and where concepts are made ready to produce action.

As an example, think of a songwriter driving from San Francisco to Los Angeles. Alone in her car, she becomes aware that she is humming a melody that has been unconsciously replaying in her mind. She imagines a catchy refrain, which she applies to the melody and sings to herself. Words and complementary parts keep coming to her. Soon everything is there. A couple hours into her drive, she has a song. The *creative* process has occurred. The song now exists. She's even given it a name. Several hours later, she gets to her hotel. Before she records the new song, she has to *arrange* it. This is the step in which the thought is formally organized. The verses are put in order, the tempo is established, an introduction and an ending are fixed, and only then is the song ready to be made into a recording. The creative thought gives the song its existence. Writing it down and arranging the song gives it form. Recording or performing it gives it physical shape and size and makes it real. All of these are connected yet separate events.

As the symbolism of Kabbalah developed over time, the "separation" between *Ein Sof* and material reality grew, in scope and complexity. In describing the physical world—the earth, the planets, light, etc.— kabbalists reflected, to the best of their own abilities, a rational picture of the universe as it would have been understood between the twelfth and fifteenth centuries. The opinions of Plato and Aristotle still carried great intellectual authority, and Neoplatonism brought a significant influence on Jewish, Christian, and Muslim philosophy. Different Greek models of a three part world, would, in essence, be represented in Kabbalah.* The three distinct acts of generativity—creation, formation, and making—became entire "worlds" to themselves. To them, a fourth "world" was added—*Atzilut*, the World of Emanation, higher and more sublime than the other three.

These four *worlds* symbolically account for the metaphysical "distance" from *Heaven* to *Earth*. Each world reflects the system above it, albeit with decreasing clarity and fidelity. Starting from the perfectly divine, they become successively coarser and less spiritual, until finally, a physical world is produced. The two uppermost worlds, *Atzilut* and *Beri'ah*, represent the incomprehensible *Will* and the unbodied *Thought*; two intellectual realms. The two lowermost, *Yetzirah* and *Asiyyah*, represent *Speech* and *Action*; two physical developments. Author and translator Avinoam Fraenkel explains:

> "The [worlds] describe a process through which a desire is convert-
> ed into action. The desire . . . stimulates the kernel of the idea of how
> to action the desire, i.e. *Atzilut*. The kernel of the idea is expanded
> upon through analytical thought, i.e. *Beriya*. The analyzed thought
> is then expressed as a spoken command, i.e. *Yetzirah*...The spoken
> command is heeded and actioned, i.e. *Asiya*." (Fraenkel, 612)

This depiction of the world being brought from nothing, symbolizes the creative process by which ideas become reality. A desire to see a change, leads to a thought of how it could be. The thought is defined

---

* The three "worlds" of Plotinus were the worlds of *Intellect, Soul*, and *Nature*, while the Aristo-
telian model gave the three "worlds" of *Separate Intelligences, Spheres*, and *Earth* see Tishby, vol.
II, p. 555

and stated clearly, and finally, it is made real by action. The *Earth*, after it was *created*, was still unformed. This symbolizes that a thought, after being willed into existence, must possess a clear and refined form, before it can be a suitable call to action.

Another instance of the three creative words, again used together, provides a practical point. '*I form light and I create darkness. I make peace*" (*Isaiah 45:7*). Kabbalah emphasizes that creation is intellectual, it's a product of thought. Following the first creative act, *the earth was void* (*Genesis 1:2*) and *darkness was upon the face of the deep* (ibid). The intellectual process of thinking or imagining something, even the greatest thought ever imagined—even the thought that created the universe— produces nothing tangible on its own. *I create darkness* (*Isaiah 45:7*). According to the kabbalistic process, the step after *creation* is *formation*. The verse in Isaiah continues, *I form light* (ibid). Fittingly, in Genesis, the third verse introduces *light*. *Let there be light* (*Genesis 1:3*), that is, let the process of *formation* commence.

Desires and thoughts, if they are ever to matter in the real world, must find their form in those words which can be made into actions. Masonic formation is, very literally, the process of learning and understanding the symbols and ceremonies of Freemasonry. It consists, both symbolically and practically, of refining our "thoughts" into the "right words." This is first true in a literal sense. Masons do, by these efforts, often develop skills that improve their ability to speak and communicate more clearly and effectively. It's also true in a figurative sense, where masonic formation provides form and structure to the more generalized idea of "being a mason." From the unformalized thought of being a freemason, to the deliberate specification of how those ideas are expressed.

Light

The *world* of formation, *yetzirah*, is sometimes described as a world of speech. In Genesis, when "*the Earth was without form,*" (*Genesis 1:2*) God *speaks* the solution. *God said, "Let there be light."* (*ibid. 3*) Combining this idea with the verse from Isaiah, "*I form light,*" kabbalists concluded that God *formed* the light by speaking. *God said, "Let there be light" and there was light.* The world of formation, therefore, is a world of speech.

Zohar I, 16b, Parashat Be-Reshit

> God said, "Let there be light!" And there was light. (Genesis 1:3)—
> Here begins the discovery of hidden treasures: how the world was
> created in detail. For until here was general, and afterward general
> returns, constituting general-particular-general.

The symbolic introduction of *light*, into one's personal journey, allows the "discovery of hidden treasures." Everybody lives a life of manifest blessings and misfortune, light and darkness, joy and sadness. The creation account in Genesis continues "*And God saw the light, that it was good. And He separated the light from the darkness*" (*Genesis 1:4*). It doesn't say God saw the darkness was *bad*, only that the light was *good*. As easy as it may be to focus on the negative, remember even the ability to identify what's bad, begins with a recognition of what is good. Light is good and darkness is *not* good. Any understanding humans have of what is bad, is, in reality, a recognition that something good *could* be there, but isn't.

From Darkness, Light

Light and dark aren't opposite *forces*, they are opposite *conditions*. Opposite forces are like two armies at war. Each is capable of advancing and capturing the territory of the other. Opposite *conditions* indicate the presence or absence of a single force or quality, in this case, light. Simply put, light can undo darkness, but the inverse is not true; darkness cannot be marshaled to overcome the light. This is an important detail of the masonic symbol of light. A hole cannot be made larger or smaller by adding or removing emptiness, but only by adding or removing sand. Darkness, like a hole, has no substance of its own, but is a void, which can only be filled by adding light.

In the previous passage is a reference to another Hebrew tradition. Known as *Kelal ufrat ukhal*—generality, particularity, and generality—it applies to a rabbinical teaching concerning the application of biblical law.[41] This tradition, known within observant Judaism, has relevance to freemasons as a symbolic tool for obtaining perspective. Each person, and every attribute they display, is an example of a larger idea. Every individual is a representation of the more general idea of *a person*. Similarly every trait and characteristic that makes up someone's personality, is an example of a more general idea. A kind act embodies the greater idea of kindness. Because you know the larger concept, you recognize the specific example. This is from general to particular.

Conversely, by coming to know yourself, you gain a better understanding of all people. Through knowing your own experiences, thoughts, feelings, and tendencies, you recognize and understand those same things in other individuals and groups. That is particular back to general.

He created "six"

I'll now explain a concept briefly mentioned earlier. The opening expression of the Bible is the single Hebrew word בראשית (*Bereshit*), *in the beginning*. The common translation is achieved by reading the prefix ב (*bet*), which means *in* or *by way of*, in front of the word ראשית (*reshit*), *beginning*. However, ancient scriptures were often without punctuation or word-spacing, so kabbalists may read the single word, instead, as two words, ברא שית (*bara shit*), *Created six*. Who created six? The implied subject—the *He* who created six—is intentionally left out, unspoken as a symbol of the ineffability and unknown nature of *Ein Sof*.

The *six*, are the *sephirot* from *Chesed* to *Yesod*. Specifically and in order they are: *Chesed* (mercy), *Gevurah* (strength), *Tif'eret* (beauty), *Netzach* (endurance), *Hod* (glory), and *Yesod* (foundation). Central among these is *Tif'eret*, to which all the others are directly connected, and which is often referred to as a proxy for the entire group of six. The symbol of *Tif'eret* representing all six is reinforced by the fact that it is the *sixth* sephirah.* This symbolism is augmented further by the association of the letters of the divine name, where *vav* (ו), with a numerical value of six, is associated with *Tif'eret* and "the six."

Zohar I, 3b, Haqdamat Sefer ha-Zohar

> Rabbi Yudai said, "What is (*Be-reshit*)? With Wisdom. This is the Wisdom on which the world stands—through which one enters hidden, high mysteries. Here were engraved six vast, supernal dimensions, from which everything emerges, from which issued six springs and streams, flowing into the immense ocean. This is (*bara shit*), *created six*, created from here. Who created them? The unmentioned, the hidden unknown."

---

* Counting from *Keter*, *Tif'eret* is the sixth *sephirah*.

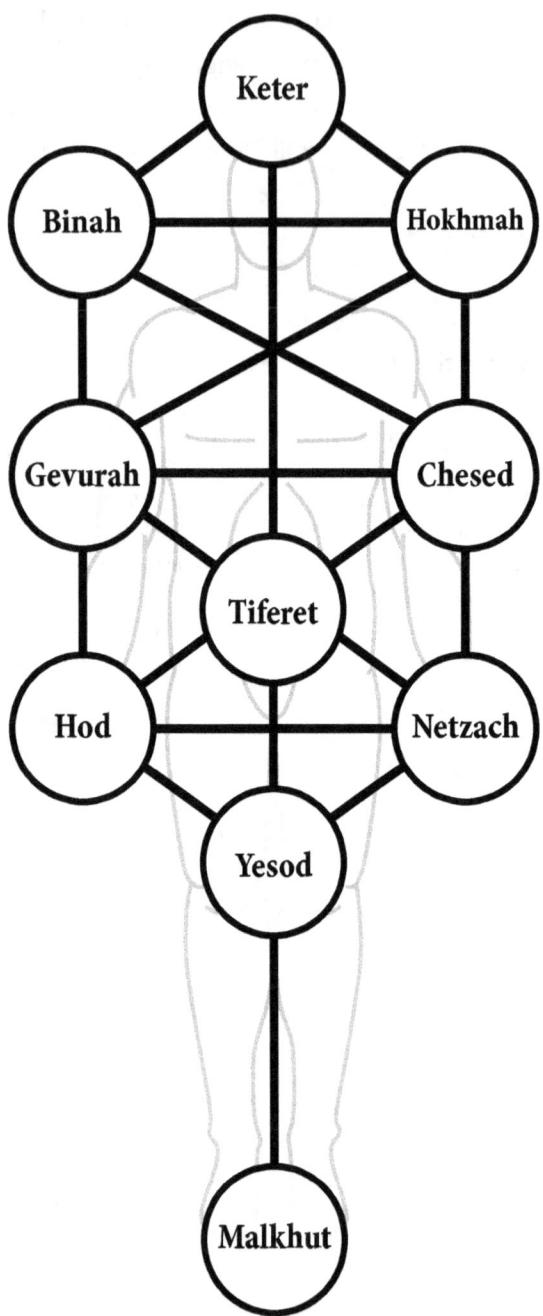

Adam Kadmon, the supernal man, represented by the sephirot.

The Pillars of the World

Previous sections referred to *left* and *right* in a symbolic context. The very idea of *left* and *right* refers to an object's physical position relative to another object. Though the *sephirot* don't exist in physical space, the symbolic *Etz Chaim*, or *Tree of Life*, illustrates how their relation to each other is most typically conceptualized. In this arrangement, the *sephirot* assume a rank and file with a top-down hierarchy and an arrangement into columns or

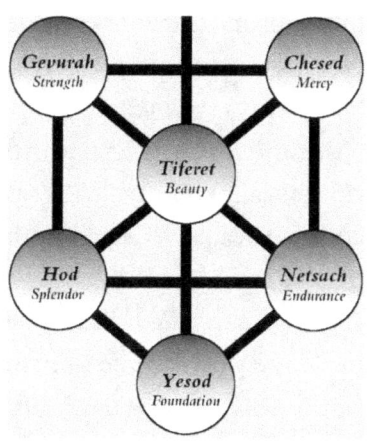

The six sephirot from *Chesed* to *Yesod*, surrounding and including *Tiferet*.

pillars.[42] Despite being commonly used alongside *above/below* symbolism, *left/right* symbolism is essentially different.

The differences are subtle but shouldn't be overlooked. The *world above* models what should be and the *world below* exemplifies that model as closely as possible. *Above* and *below*, therefore, in the critical details *resemble* each other, even if not perfectly. *Right/left* symbolism, differently, is not reflective, it is complementary. The two parts *do not* resemble each other in the critical details. Each possesses, and is able to provide, a specific contribution which the other needs but cannot supply for itself. In a previous example, the verse, "*My hand founded the earth, and My right hand spread out heaven*" (Isaiah 48:13), gave a peek at *right/left* symbolism. That passage, referred specifically to the right and left hands. The sephirah *Chesed*, Mercy, is the "*right hand*" and *Gevurah*, Strength, also called *Din*, Judgment, is symbolized by the "*left hand.*"

Religious mythology tends to anthropomorphism, that is, describing deity in human terms. Throughout the Bible, are references to the bodily parts of God. The mention of his *hands* made in Isaiah is just one example.

Time and again, the Bible mentions the *eyes, ears, feet, fingers,* and *face* of God. To rational critics of tradition, this was not only illogical, it was blasphemy. The kabbalists turned again to the *sephirot*. The *sephirot*, they explained, are not only the divine model for the created universe, they are also the divine *image* after which human beings were created. "*Let us make mankind in our image and after our own likeness . . .*" (*Genesis 1:26*). Any mention of the body of God should be understood as symbolically referring to the *sephirot*. The highest three constituted the crowned head, the next three the arms and torso, and the bottom three the legs and lower body.[43] *Malkhut* is his footstool. The inclusion of the supernal man, *Adam Kadmon*, as the model of the universe, effectively made every person into a microcosm, a miniature version of the whole world. This theme is frequently revisited in Kabbalah, particularly in portions of the *Zohar* known as the *Idrot* and the *Sifra D'tzniuta*.

Between *above* and *below* there is a clear and intentional expression of subordination or preeminence. That is to say, *below* can never challenge *above* for "ascendancy" or gain "the upper hand," so to speak. This type of relationship is frequently expressed by *cause/effect* or *parent/child* symbolism. The *child* can never beget the *parent* like the *effect* can't precede the *cause*. *Left* and *right* symbolism does not include this implication. Unlike the *above/below* arrangement where the two parts relate according to how one resembles the other, *left* and *right* exist apart from each other, as independent concepts, and their relationship concerns how they are *not alike*. *Right* and *left* are, in many symbolic examples, a pair of opposites, which counteract each other, such as light and dark, hot and cold, or wet and dry. In other cases, *right* and *left* represent couples which interact to enhance, refine, or regulate the other.

The *Tree of Life* is the classic depiction of Kabbalah's defining symbols and also of this, perhaps its most central tenet, here explained by Isaiah Tishby:

> "The preservation of the world, therefore, depends on the mingling and moderation of opposing forces. The foundations of life and of ordered direction in the world are . . . liable to fall at any moment.

"... When the spirit disappears they all quiver and tremble, the world quakes." (Job 9:6) Only a single step separates the conflict of harmonious love, which sustains the world, from the conflict of divisive hatred, which plunges the world into destruction and disaster. Herein lies the tremendous responsibility of mankind, for it is man that has the wherewithal to harmonize the opposing powers and to effect a balance between them, and it is his actions that can turn the scale toward innocence or guilt. The consequences of man's actions are not confined to the reward or punishment that might come to him personally, for there is a kind of collective responsibility. The actions of individuals are combined together, and it is their total influence that determines the way in which the whole world is governed ... Man's involvement in the direction of the world, which is one of the basic tenets of kabbalistic doctrine, imposes upon him a very heavy responsibility. He has continually to see himself as part of the complex of the opposing forces in the Godhead and in the cosmos, and it is part of his task to help to moderate the extremes, and so to bring peace to the Godhead and to the world. On the other hand, he must beware of increasing the power of the opposing forces, and so feeding the fire of a destructive conflict." (Tishby, vol. I, p. 428–429)

This, *"to harmonize the opposing powers and to effect a balance between them"* is also the work of freemasons. Generally speaking, this work is divided into two tasks. Masons seek, first, balance in their own life, and after that, order and peace within the group. Without some semblance of the former, there is little hope of contributing to the latter. Freemasonry makes this type of harmony a priority in its lodges and gatherings. While no group is perfect, for the most part, it achieves this goal, and the typical masonic affair is friendly and free of acrimony. Many lodges are, in fact, close-knit groups, whose members are the truest of friends. In today's society, politics and social division foster violent animosity around nearly every issue. Even within groups, primary self-interest and a broad disregard for civility, mean disagreements are generally hostile and unforgiving. Finding balance or harmony is as difficult now as perhaps it has ever been.

Balance is not achieved by being so perfectly situated that nothing can disturb or move you, but instead balance is constantly being regained.

Balance is an ongoing process of resettling and reestablishing yourself upright. A person is never so much *well balanced* as they are *balancing well*. Life is dynamic and unpredictable. Upset and disruption are unavoidable. Taking the path necessary for progress often involves launching ourselves forward, either confident or hopeful that we'll find our balance again after every step. Kabbalah uses *left/right* symbolism to express this balance, mainly in two ways, both of which are alluded to by Tishby above. "*[It] is part of his task to help to moderate the extremes, and so to bring peace to the Godhead and to the world.*" In one application, the two forces are interdependent, combining to produce something positive. This symbolism is noticed plainly in Kabbalah's tradition of *Hokhmah* and *Binah* as symbolic *Father* and *Mother*, and hidden in the biblical story of *Adam and Eve*. In symbolism of this type, the right, *male* side provides a *thought* or a *seed*, which the *female* left side *understands*, *nourishes to life*, or otherwise completes. *Left* and *right* in these cases symbolize complementary and cooperative forces, and their union is productive.

Another type of *left/right* symbolism, involves two independent forces who are not cooperative but are essentially at odds with each other. These are the symbols Tishby alludes to saying, "*on the other hand, he must beware of increasing the power of the opposing forces, and so feeding the fire of a destructive conflict.*" In this version of *left/right* symbolism, the two sides temper, limit, or otherwise mitigate each other to prevent either from becoming harmful. These are symbols like *fire* and *water*. It would be imprecise to say that fire is *the opposite* of water, but the presence of one certainly reduces the effect of the other. Both, however, are required to the necessary degree, at the appropriate time and place, and neither can be entirely eliminated. A balance must be maintained and neither side can ever assume too much influence.

Fire and Water

Conflict, interdependence, harmony and balance are all present in the symbolic *Tree of Life*. The *sephirot* are arranged in three vertical columns called *pillars*. The right column, often called the *Pillar of Mercy*, consists of *Hokhmah*, *Chesed*, and *Netzach*. The column on the left, known as the *Pillar of Severity* or *Judgment*, includes *Binah*, *Gevurah*, and *Hod*. The central pillar has four *sephirot*—*Keter*, *Tif'eret*, *Yesod*, and *Malkhut*—and reconciles the left and right with each other. To freemasons, who pattern their lodges symbolically after the biblical Temple of King Solomon, the symbolism of pillars is fitting. The pillars of *Mercy* and *Judgment*, just mentioned, are also known by other names. Atop the right column sits *Hokhmah*, so the right one is sometimes called

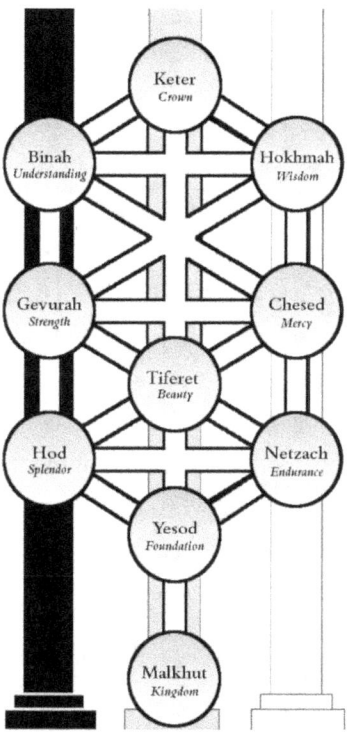

The *sephirot* are arranged in three vertical rows, imagined as pillars. The "Pillar of Mercy" on the right and the "Pillar of Severity" on the left are balanced by the "Pillar of Beauty" in the middle.

Pillar of Wisdom. The left column, taking its name from *Gevurah*, is called *Pillar of Strength*. The central pillar is named after *Tif'eret*, *Pillar of Beauty*. The *Zohar* is inconsistent in describing the number of pillars that symbolically *support* the world, in different places describing various numbers. Since three is the number illustrated by the *Tree of Life*, and is symbolically relevant to Freemasonry, it's logical to continue with the following example which refers, although indirectly, to three pillars.

Zohar I, 77a, Lekh Lekha

For when the blessed Holy One created the world, He made the heavens out of fire and water commingled as one, but they did not congeal. Afterward they congealed and endured through supernal spirit. Thence He sowed the world to stand upon pillars, those pillars standing only through that spirit. When the spirit disappears they all quiver and tremble, the world quakes, as is written: *Who shakes the earth from her place, and her pillars tremble* (Job 9:6).

Now the *Zohar* explains that when the world was created, not only was the earth still *unformed*, but the heavens were *uncongealed* as well. *Spirit*, however, repaired that problem and the heavens endured. Seeing the heavens stabilized, the Great Architect designed the earth to stand upon three pillars. The kabbalistic symbolism of the heavens being made from *fire* and *water*—perhaps the epitome of the "mutually limiting" type of *right/left* symbolism—begins with a play on words. The Hebrew word for *fire*, אש (*esh*), is combined with the word for *water*, מים (*mayim*) to produce the word for *heavens*, שמים (*shamayim*). As was mentioned in the preceding section, *water* and *fire* are symbols of the sephirot *Chesed* and *Gevurah*. The *Zohar* offers this additional dynamic account.

Zohar I, 86b - 87a, Parashat Lekh Lekha

"And Melchizedek, king of Salem . . . " (Genesis 14:18)[*]

Rabbi Shim'on opened, "*In Salem is His tabernacle* . . . (Psalms 76:3). Come and see: When it arose in the will of the blessed Holy One to create the world, He generated a single flame of a lamp of impenetrable darkness and blew spark against spark. It darkened and ignited. From the recesses of the abyss He generated a single drop and joined them as one, thereby creating the world.

"The flame ascended, crowned on the left; the drop ascended, crowned on the right. Culminating in one another, they exchanged places, one to this side, one to that, the descendent ascending, the ascendent descending, both intertwining. Between them issued a perfect spirit so those two sides turned into one; it was placed between them—they were crowned with one another."

---

[*] The full verse of Genesis 14:18 reads "*And Melchizedek, king of Salem, brought forth bread and wine.*" Here however, R. Shim'on is only concerned with the first portion.

Nothing about the *Zohar* is straightforward. In this example, Shim'on endeavors to explain Genesis 14:18 (*"And Melchizedek, King of Salem . . . "*). He opens with a line from Psalms 76:3, *"In Salem is His tabernacle."* Common between the two verses is the word *Salem*. The Hebrew root, *sh-l-m* (ש-ל-מ), means *completion* (*shalem* שלם) or *perfect* (*shalaym* שלם), and can also mean *peace* (*shalom* שלם,שלום). This versatility is played on throughout the explanation. The *flame* formed a column on the *"left"* and the *drop* formed one on the *"right"* however, as was explained, the two do not *congeal*. The chaotic interaction between *fire* and *water* is mediated by *spirit*, the Hebrew word for which, *ruach* (רוח), is also the plain word for *wind* or *air*.

While Kabbalah shares many symbols with other traditions, Masonry included, its interpretations are uniquely its own.[44] The *flame* and the *drop* from this example illustrate a mutually limiting idea of *right* and *left*. This concept is at the heart of a kabbalistic tenet concerning divine *Judgment* being tempered by perfect *Mercy*. The particularly descriptive imagery has *Judgment* enflame and rise higher, while *Mercy* pours down and extinguishes. A measure of balance is achieved through the direct and limiting relationship of one to the other. The greater the *fire*, the more *water* is needed to abate it. Without the influence of the other, each would be destructive.

An important point made earlier, is that the kabbalists developed their symbolic explanations to accord with the prevailing understanding of the world at the time. In the symbolism of the previous examples, there are obvious references to the ancient Greek idea of the four elements of nature, the belief in which was still current at the time the *Zohar* was written. Along with the *earth,* there are *the heavens* which are made up of *fire, water,* and *air*. Aristotle was particularly exalted in Medieval and early Modern thinking and his influence can be seen in parts of the *Zohar*. To the four elements, Aristotle associated two qualities, moisture and heat, which he delineated along the extremes of each. Four essential characteristics—dry, moist, hot, and cold—were assigned to the four elements. Accordingly, earth was dry and cold, while fire was dry and hot. Water, directly opposed to fire, was moist and cold. Possessing the heat of fire and the moisture of water, the natural reconciliation of those two was air, the Hebrew word for which, *ruach* (רוח), is throughout the Bible, most commonly translated as *spirit*.

This is a very good example of how the kabbalists managed to fit their traditional symbols (*the words of the Bible*) with new concepts (*Ein Sof, sephirot,* etc.) that supported their moral doctrinal teachings (*mercy should temper judgment*) and matched it to contemporary rational thinking (*the relationships of the four elements to each other*). Salient is the fact that what was considered "rational thinking" in the Middle Ages, would not be today. Society changes. This is the point. Ideas develop into different ideas. In any society, the beliefs and language are bound to change over time. The kabbalists faced the challenges of such changes nearly a thousand years ago and Freemasonry today should learn from that success. By displaying and encouraging a creative approach to examining and understanding them, Masonry's symbols can be to current and future generations, as meaningful as they have ever been.

Adam and Eve

Whereas *fire* and *water* are mutually limiting, *male* and *female* are mutually enabling. The relationship of women and men, even if historically and contemporarily fraught, has, nonetheless, long been a symbol of fruitful cooperation. Their interdependence and unique compatibility have often been applied to the symbols of *right* and *left*. The right and left hands, though each is differently capable, are used together to greater effect than either could be by itself. With the input of the other, both participate in something greater than what either might do by themselves.

The Bible account of Adam and Eve, obscured for most by glaring mistranslations, contains an early example of the two sides symbolically associated with *male* and *female*. In the familiar version of the story, God fashions Eve, the first woman, from a "rib" of Adam, the first man.

However, the Hebrew word *tsela* (צלע), which appears in the Bible over forty times, is only translated as "rib" in this one case. In practically every other instance, the word is simply translated as "side." Also of note, the Hebrew word *adam* (אדם), is translated throughout the first several chapters of the Bible simply as "man," referring generally to the human species; literally *mankind* or *humanity*. This usage is clearly seen, for example, when it's written *"God created man in His image . . . male and female He created them"* (Genesis 1:27-28). However, toward the end of the third chapter, the Hebrew word *adam* begins to be rendered as the proper name *Adam*.

A modern understanding of science and prehistoric humanity makes the literal story of Adam and Eve unlikely as an historical account. The "rib story" is a perfect example of a tradition becoming entirely meaningless to contemporary society. No longer possessing value as either a literal account or a moralistic fable, it's now one of the bizarre and inexplicable scenes that has led recent generations to increasingly reject the Bible as unreliable at best and reprehensible at worst. However, the same tale is remarkably different as a depiction of women composing one "side" of "humankind." It instead tells a story of the complementary nature of men and women and, more generally, the male and female aspects of life and existence. In Masonry, notions of cooperation and compatibility are maintained in various symbols traditionally tied to the *male/female* symbolism; the *sun* and *moon*, for example. Described in an earlier section, the receptive capacity of the *moon* and the generative power of the *sun* were classically symbolized, respectively, as feminine and masculine attributes. The *Adam and Eve* story, as it's been now explained, is repeated in the following passage from the *Zohar* with the characters of sun and moon as the symbolic *male* and *female*. Male and female begin as two *sides of a single entity*, who are then separated, reoriented, and rejoined to each other.

Zohar I, 20a, Parashat Be-Reshit

"*God made the two great lights* (Genesis 1:16). *Made* - enhancement and arrayal of all, fittingly. *The two great lights*—at first a single bond, mystery of the name complete as one: יהוה אלהים (YHVH Elohim), though not revealed, rather in a manner concealed . . . Similarly, *the two lights*, both ascending as one . . . The moon was uneasy with the sun, ashamed in its presence. The moon said, "*Where do you pasture your sheep? Where do you let them rest at noon?* (Song of Songs 1:7). How can a little lamp shine at noon? . . . So she diminished herself . . . From that point on she has light only from the sun.

The *Zohar* refers to two more traditions in explaining this verse. In one, the meaning of the verse is questioned.[45] 'It is written: *God made the two great lights*, and it is written in the same verse: *the greater light . . . and the lesser light.*' (*Genesis 1:16*) The explanation repeats the idea that the two sides were once united. Their unity is symbolized by two divine names used together, *YHVH Elohim*, rendered in English as *The* LORD *God.*[*] The second tradition relates the various divine names found in the Bible to specific *sephirot*. In the current example, the use of the *sun* and *moon* as symbols makes it apparent that the name *YHVH* symbolizes *Tif'eret* and *Elohim* refers to *Malkhut*, the emblematic *moon.*[46]

The explanation is a tale of humility. In the full brightness of the sun, the moon feels its contribution inadequate. Questioning its role, it resigns itself to retire. It refers to itself by a verse from the biblical Song of Songs, '*Where do you pasture your sheep? Where do you let them rest at noon?*' (Songs 1:7). It expresses its feelings of inadequacy with the rhetorical question, "*How can a little lamp shine at noon?*" In some accounts, the moon is ordered to stand down, in others it reduces itself voluntarily. In either case, "*she diminished herself*" and "*had only the light of the sun.*" The moon's humility, of course, is rewarded in the end. Recognized for its patience and propriety, it's elevated to the position always intended for it, equal to the sun. The Kabbalist refers to the Book of Psalms:

---

[*] The Hebrew divine name YHVH is never pronounced. When reading aloud, the word *Adonai*, Lord, is spoken in its place. This practice is maintained in most occurrences in most written translations.

Zohar I, 31a

Day illumines night, but night does not shine until that time of which it is written "*the night shall shine as the day; the darkness shall be as the light*" (Psalms 139:12).

The waning of the moon was made to symbolize humility. The waxing of the moon symbolized the reward of that humility, the full realization of your highest potential. The biblical prophet Isaiah seems to confirm it: "*Your sun will no longer go down; neither will your moon wane: for the LORD will be to you the light of the world*" (*Isaiah 60:20*). The symbolic interpretation provides a very important lesson. The moon was not created to be inferior to the sun. However, it accepts its appointed role until the time comes for it to occupy its eventual place. Masons, also, must increase their light until such a time when they are called upon to share it.

Sephirah	Hebrew Name	English Translation
Malkhut	Adonai	Lord
Yesod	El Shaddai	God Almighty
Hod	Elohim Tsvaot	God of Armies
Netzach	YHVH Tsvaot	LORD of Armies
Tif'eret	YHVH	LORD[47]
Gevurah	Elohim	God(s)
Chesed	El	God
Binah	YHV	Jahu
Hokhmah	YH	Jah
Keter	Ehyeh	I am

The divine names as they correspond to the *sephirot* according to Joseph Gikatilla's *the Gates of Light*.

The Names of God

Alluded to several times already, the names of God are important symbols in Kabbalah. Most English speaking readers of the Bible are unaware of just how many Hebrew words are generically translated as *God*. Same with the word *Lord*. The relatively well-known examples like *Elohim, Adonai, Jehovah*, etc. are just a few of the biblical names for God.

Modern bible researchers generally attribute the large variety of names to the fusion of different traditions in the development of the bible literature. The leading theory suggests the "gods" of previously competing mythologies were merged over time into the God of the Bible. Kabbalists, however, many centuries earlier provided a different explanation: each of the divine names refers to the *sephirot*. These *names* would largely be organized and explained by Rabbi Joseph Gikatilla in perhaps his most important work, *the Gates of Light*, written in Spain around the same time as the *Zohar*. The table on the previous page shows the correspondence of the divine names to the *sephirot* according to him.

The Four Letter Name of God

Of all the names and titles of God, there is one that is special. The ineffable four-letter name of God, יהוה (YHVH), called the tetragrammaton, is set apart in Jewish tradition. The distinction of this word is maintained also by Christianity, which shares the Hebrew scriptures with Judaism.[48] YHVH is not an honorific or moniker but is held to be the true *name* of God, so holy that the word is never pronounced. When reading scripture aloud, the word *Adonai* is pronounced in its place.* Christians preserve this tradition in text, rendering the word as *the Lord*.

The passage concerning Melchizedek, begun in the previous example, is concluded here with Rabbi Shim'on resolving his opening reference, *In Salem is his Tabernacle (Psalms 76:3)*.

---

* There is one case where it is replaced with "Elohim."

Zohar I, 86b - 87a, Parashat Lekh Lekha (cont.)

> Then peace prevailed above, peace below, and the rung stabilized. ה (*he*) was crowned with ו (*vav*), ו (*vav*) with ה (*he*), then ה (*he*) ascended, bound in a perfect bond. Then: *Melchizedek, king of Salem,* actually *king of perfection*, indeed, a king ruling over perfection!"

The play on the Hebrew word שלם (*shalem*), *Salem*, continues. By this word—the name of a well-known place literally meaning *completion, perfection*, or *peace*—the rabbi refers back to his opening statement. *Fire* and *water* were reconciled by the spirit, then he says, "*peace* prevailed above, *peace* below, and the *rung* stabilized." Peace, above and below; again the word for peace is *shalem*, which also means perfect or complete. The passage may therefore be understood to refer to the "perfection" above and the "completeness" below, by which the entire structure is made solid. The *rung*, is a symbol of *Tif'eret*, also

According to mystical tradition, the four-letter name of God corresponds to the ten *sephirot*, and to all of creation.

known as *the heavens*, where the top rung of Jacob's ladder is set.

A series of unexplained references to letters of the Hebrew alphabet follows. Shim'on relates a kabbalistic tradition where the four letters of the ineffable name, יהוה (*yod, he, vav, he*), represent all ten *sephirot*. The first letter, *yod*, not mentioned in this passage, refers to *Keter* and *Hokhmah*. Shim'on, however, concerns himself here only with the other three, *he, vav,* and *he*. These, according to the tradition, refer respectively to *Binah, Tif'eret* or the "*six*," and *Malkhut*. *Malkhut*, the lower *he*, is "crowned by" *vav*, *Tif'eret*, which is "crowned by" *Binah*, the upper *he*, connecting them from top to bottom "*in perfect bond.*"*

So "*in Salem is His Tabernacle*" (*Psalms 76:3*) can be understood instead as "in *perfection* is His Tabernacle." *His Tabernacle*, the site of God's presence among the people in the wilderness, is *Malkhut*. Eventually, the Rabbi enigmatically explains that "*Melchizedek, King of Salem*" (*Genesis 14:18*), also refers to *Malkhut*. The name Melchizedek means "righteous king" or "king of righteousness." The name *Malkhut* means *kingdom* but the *sephirah* is also called by the nickname *zedek*, (righteousness). This means that both references, the Tabernacle and Melchizedek, symbolically refer to *Malkhut*, the Divine Presence—the *king of righteousness* presiding over *complete perfection*.

Upper Judgment and Lower Judgment

In the earlier example concerning the two great lights, the divine name *Elohim* was associated with *Malkhut*. However, the name *Elohim* is usually assigned to *Gevurah*, also known as *Din*, Judgment. The borrowing of the name *Elohim* signifies *Malkhut's* relationship to Judgment. Another Kabbalistic tradition involves *Upper Judgment* and *Lower Judgment*. In a nutshell, Lower Judgment is the imperfect and "impatient" judgment that governs this world. It is, at times, too severe, and at other times, too lenient. So it is sometimes that people appear to be rewarded for terrible behavior, while others seem to be punished unfairly. Upper Judgment is the perfect, "long-suffering" judgment awaiting in the world that is coming, where all kindness and service will be accounted for and every person will truly receive a just reward.

The practical message is, every action we take has consequences, both immediately and in an unforeseeable time and place. This law of cause and effect is both physical and philosophical. There are immediate consequences to missteps. In the physical world they can result in injuries and damage. Tripping sometimes ends in falling and the laws of nature

---

* Again, *Salem* means perfect.

are strictly enforced by the ground. These missteps, frequent in childhood and decreasing with maturity, are symbolic of those missteps that occur in our relationships, to which the law equally applies. The immediate consequences of these may often be rightly compared to having tripped and fallen. This is the Lower Judgment.

It may be however, that the missteps which were immediately punished by Lower Judgment, are viewed differently in the long run. There are many proverbs about falling down and getting back up that allude to the value in learning from mistakes. We often learn a great deal from falling down. In the end, every experience of falling down results in growth, without which we never realize any greater perfection. This is the Upper Judgment. Patience allows for perspective to grow and accommodate the entire picture. Much of what is judged harshly by Lower Judgment, is redeemed in time by Upper Judgment. The opposite statement is also true. Much of what is allowed by Lower Judgment will finally be held to account by Upper Judgment.

Lower Judgment, however imperfect, is not avoidable. Just as falling and hitting the ground is judged immediately by the laws of matter and physics, we must act and react. We don't always have the luxury of waiting to see how things work out. The symbols teach that the impatient judgment required in this world is imperfect and often will be corrected in time. Always be willing to reconsider past decisions in the greater light of the current situation. Upper Judgment, being perfect, is only an idea, but it's an idea that's available for humans to use as a model. All people, particularly masons, should aspire to be as patient as possible in passing judgment; willing to see how things may change, hopeful that wrongs can be righted, and fair and forgiving when they are.

Lower Judgment will always exist with Upper Judgment. Lower Judgment is your immediate response in every situation while Upper Judgment is your later assessment of that experience, reflected in the greater context of your total life. Prudence hopes to bring the Lower Judgment closer in line with the Upper Judgment. Try to imagine the long-term ramifications of what you do before you do it. Understand every experience will be one you ultimately reflect on, and aim to have as few regrets as possible. As you consider the immediate consequences of your actions, also try to imagine how your present actions will look to your future self. Perhaps you are immediately reluctant to do something, but you believe it will be good for you in the long run. Or conversely you're tempted to do something, but you know it will be something you're not proud of. Considering the long-term effects of everything you do will lead to fewer regrets and improve your chance at future happiness.

Painting by artist David Friedman entitled *Psalm 107*. The entire verse is written out in a pattern known in Sacred Geometry as the *Seed of Life*.

East to West, North to South

The passage through life has already been symbolically marked out in *time*, signified by three parts of the day; morning, midday, and evening. This symbolism represents the general idea of progress from a beginning, through a middle, to an end. For the vast majority of the earth's population living in the Northern Hemisphere, the sun daily traversed the southern sky. Rising in the east, the sun climbed to a peak before descending and setting in the west. The sun's journey through space from east to west, marked out, in a visible way, the advance of time, from morning to evening, and symbolically, the progress of life from youth to old age.

As with *above/below* and *left/right* symbolism, there are numerous symbolic interpretations of *east* and *west*. Progress from a beginning in the east to an end in the west commonly represents the stages of life from the dawn of childhood to the sunset of late age. This, famously, is the substance of the earlier mentioned *Riddle of the Sphinx*. Within Freemasonry, this symbolism is obvious. However the emblematic path from *east* to *west* concerns more than one's physical life. The symbolic journey first and more directly, involves each person's search for *light*, which emerges in the east and reposes in the west. Light is a symbol of *truth* and so the east symbolizes the *source* of truth and the west symbolizes the *reception* of truth.

The symbolic use of *east, west, north*, and *south* is perhaps more prominent in Masonry than it is in Kabbalah. However, it's not absent from Kabbalah. According to Hebrew tradition, the *south* symbolizes the *right*, and the *north* aligns with the *left*, resulting in an east-facing orientation. Moving clockwise, the journey from *east* to *west* passes through the *south*, and the return trip from *west* to *east* moves through the *north*.

This symbolizes the continuous nature of learning. As mentioned, most inhabitants of earth for most of history only ever saw the sun in the southern sky. The north became a symbol of darkness. With light being a symbol of knowledge or truth, darkness is a symbol of ignorance or falseness. So a journey from *not-knowing* to *knowing* is metaphorically traveled through the dark *north*, with the hope of arriving at the source of light in the *east*. From there the journey continues. Light, always moving through the *south*, grows to an apex but begins to diminish as it approaches the west. This signifies that each advance in our personal knowledge and understanding, starts with an increase that soon reveals that there is much more to learn. Hence the well-worn paraphrase of Aristotle, *the more you know, the more you realize how much you don't know.*

Learning is a cycle. Each new answer brings with it many more questions. So the quest for light begins groping through the symbolic dark of *not-knowing* until discovering the hopeful glimmer of the coming dawn. The faint light of *knowing* grows until it illuminates from *east* to *west*. At the pinnacle of the day, the knowledge is fullest and this is when the entire horizon can be seen. Looking back toward the dawn and the preceding night, the light of new knowledge shines into the past and answers long held questions. Looking ahead, the same light anticipates the sunset that will slowly consume it and the darkness of the new unknown that always waits just beyond the horizon. So the appearance of light is followed by a return to darkness, and the quest must forever be resumed. The search for truth, or the quest for knowledge, is never ending.

In Kabbalah, the symbolic balancing of light and dark, with their continual ebb and flow, is again represented in the story of existence. *All is one*, say the kabbalists, and every story—creation, existence, life—is a journey in search of *light*. The forces harnessed to create the universe, are the same ones that still govern its entirety, and the same ones that also shape human experience. The search for *light*, in Kabbalah, is akin to the mystical search for knowledge *of* the Divine. Whereas ancient priests and magicians were often interested in procuring knowledge *from* divinity, the concern of the mystic was to know the true nature *of* divinity. The kabbalists' idea that the physical universe is the deliberate act of a hidden Creator, revealing itself to humans, had significant implications. The material world, not identical to God was, nonetheless, a reflection of divinity. Far from the corrupt and illusory world of Gnostics and dualistic traditions, the created world of Kabbalah, though admittedly not perfect, was still the best world possible, given the limitations of material existence. Nature was not something to be despised or overcome, but was the key to unlocking the ultimate truth. By a careful observation of nature, both the structure of reality and the attributes of divinity could be known.

Zohar III, 182a, Parashat Huqqat

> *Moving toward the south, circling toward the north* (Ecclesiastes 1:6)—corresponding to what is written: *from His right hand, a fiery law for them* (Deuteronomy 33:2). *His right hand* is *south*; *a fiery law* is *north*—one included in the other.

> *Round and round goes the wind* (Ecclesiastes 1:6). This verse is difficult; it should read *Round and round goes the sun!* Well, what is this רוח (*ruach*), wind? This is *under the sun*, called רוח הקדש (*ruach ha-qodesh*), the Holy Spirit. This *ruach goes—goes around* these two sides to join the body. Thus it is written, הרוח (*ha-ruach*), *the wind*—that well-known one.

South and *north* are unambiguously identified with *right* and *left*. Rabbi Shimʿon employs an unorthodox interpretation of Deuteronomy to explain a verse from Ecclesiastes.[49] He divides the verse, *from His right hand a fiery law for them* (*Deuteronomy 33:2*), into two discrete concepts. The subject of the verse is the Torah, *the Law*, which comes from the *right hand*. However, the expression *Fiery Law* refers to *Gevurah* and the *Pillar of Fire*, the kabbalistic *left hand*. This, the rabbi suggests, emphasizes the ultimate unity of all things. *Left* and *right*, originally from an undivided whole, are reunited in the Torah, a symbolic reference to *Tifʿeret*, where all is balanced. The two sides, south and north, are just reciprocal parts of a solitary truth.

The verse from Ecclesiastes continues with the words "*round and round goes the wind.*" Rabbi Shimʿon imagines the verse should instead be written *"round and round goes the sun."* In the symbols of Kabbalah, the *sun* is another well attested reference to *Tif'eret*, ever resolving the conflict between the two sides. The rabbi asks why the verse is not, therefore, written, the *sun*, but instead is written, the *wind*. *Asking rhetorically—What is this wind?*—he gives a perplexing answer to his own question. The wind, he says, is *"under the sun."*

The book Ecclesiastes, attributed to King Solomon, is distinguished by the author's repeated use of a phrase found nowhere else in the bible; *under the sun*. With *Tif'eret* as the *sun*, the expression *under the sun* is taken to refer to *Malkhut*, symbolically situated below *Tif'eret*. In previous examples, *ruach* (spirit, air, wind), which reconciled *right* and *left,* was related to *Tif'eret*. Why now does Shim'on say *ruach* refers to *Malkhut*? Aware of the contradiction, Shim'on explains that in this case, the word is written as *ha-ruach*, *the wind*. Using the definite article *the*, implies familiarity. This isn't just any wind, this is *the wind*, the *well-known one*. Therefore, the rabbi says, *the wind*, in this case, is *Malkhut*, the *Shekinah*, who dwells with and is intimately known to the people. She *"goes around,"* or encompasses both the *left* and *right* sides, unifying them into a single body.

This may appear to be one of the frequent inconsistencies encountered in the *Zohar*, where something is said in one place which is apparently contradicted in another. However, careful consideration might suggest otherwise. In examples where the conciliatory *spirit, ruach,* refers to *Tif'eret*, the two forces being reconciled are, symbolically speaking, *Chesed* and *Gevurah*, *brotherly-love* and *strength*, the *water* and *fire* of heaven. These three, *Chesed, Gevurah*, and *Tif'eret*, form the central triad in the Tree of Life. However, Shim'on suggests this case is different. Left and right are not the *fire* and *water* of *heaven*, but *north* and *south*. Directions—*north, south, east,* and *west*—belong to geography, the charting of the *earth*. Rabbi Shim'on teaches that the balance of earthly things occurs within *Malkhut*.

The practical value is in considering this: there is no standing still. Our lives occur in a stream of constantly unfolding time. The emblematic *ebb* and *flow* of knowledge from *not-knowing* to *knowing* to *not-knowing* again, from *seeking* to *finding* to *seeking* something further, applies to all areas of life. Balance is required spiritually between hope and understanding, emotionally between desire and reason, and in our physical lives between our morals and virtues on one side and our appetites and interests on the other. However, life is in constant motion and equilibrium can be difficult to achieve. Sometimes we are strong and other times we're wanting, we improve and we decline, we're blessed and we're beset. Balance must always be maintained. By a well-planned and steady course, be confident the path through the dark leads to light, and have the courage always to push ahead across the next horizon and to whatever unknown lies there beyond.

1790 painting by John Murphy depicting the biblical story of Hiram, King of Tyre presenting gifts to King Solomon.

Wisdom, Strength, and Beauty

Masonic lodges are symbolically styled after the biblical Temple of Solomon, which famously included two pillars at its entrance. Freemasonry, therefore, involves the use of pillars both literally and figuratively. Along with physical pillars depicting those mentioned in the Bible (1 Kings 7:21, 2 Chronicles 3:17), are three metaphorical *pillars*: *Wisdom*, *Strength*, and *Beauty*.

Wisdom

Masonry adopted as their own, the *four cardinal virtues* of classical Greek philosophy.[50] These virtues are symbolically taught through the rituals, symbols, and legends of Masonry. Each mason is encouraged to practice them to the best of their ability. The virtues, in their original Greek names are *sōphrosýnē, andreía, phrónēsis*, and *dikaiosýnē*, known in English as *temperance, fortitude, prudence*, and *justice*. Most masons will immediately recognize them in this particular form. Outside of Freemasonry, these words are regularly translated in other ways. The Greek *phrónēsis*, here translated *prudence*, is commonly translated as *wisdom*.

In English, *wisdom* and *prudence* aren't exact synonyms but *prudence* is, to be sure, a type of *wisdom*. Specifically, it is *applied* wisdom. More than simply knowing right from wrong, *prudence* is choosing what is beneficial and avoiding what does harm. It's a virtue which Masonry hopes to develop and refine in its members. Prudence, like any virtue, must be performed. To *know* what is beneficial is not prudent by itself. Knowledge has to produce right behavior. It's no virtue to know better and still do what is harmful. Prudence is wisdom put into practice. Kabbalistically, it relates to the sephirah *Binah, understanding*, where abstract wisdom becomes useful as practical knowledge.[51]

Freemasons, to distinguish themselves from practicing stonemasons, refer to their enterprise as *Speculative Masonry*. This shouldn't however suggest that Freemasonry no longer includes a practical element. In a self-described "system of morality," the *work* of Freemasonry is the practice of *virtue*. Morals are believed, virtue is practiced. The overarching message of Masonry to its members is ultimately simple. At all times and to the highest degree possible, do what is right and avoid doing what is wrong.

Strength

Directly opposed to *Wisdom*, in the symbolism of Kabbalah and Masonry, is *Strength*. In Kabbalah, *Strength* and *Judgment* are embodied by the same sephirah, called interchangeably by both names. While *strength* is typically considered a positive trait, *judgment* often carries a negative connotation. In everyday usage, the word usually implies either personal criticism or a legal consequence, neither of which is particularly pleasant. In Kabbalah, *judgment* is often associated with the repercussions of bad conduct or poor decision making. Judgment, however, is better understood simply as "an appropriate response to the facts of a matter."* When your response is appropriate, your judgment is called sound, when it's not, it's called poor. Considered in this way, it's easy to see how judgment, especially sound judgment, is, truly, a *strength*.

Judgment and *strength* relate in another way. Along with sound judgment *being* a strength, judgment also *requires* strength. To have an appropriate response to the facts, one must have, first, an accurate assessment of those facts. This is often easier said than done, especially when the facts concern one's self or close associates. Finding flaws in strangers and adversaries is easy. Finding them in yourself and your friends is difficult. To be honest in those cases, and respond appropriately, takes a type of strength called *fortitude*. This is the type of strength that supports sound judgment. *Judgment* isn't qualified by the consequences it

---

* my definition

demands. What I mean is, a lenient judgment is not necessarily *good*, nor a strict one *bad*. The quality of any person's judgment is determined by how closely it reflects an appropriate response to reality. Good judgment accounts well for the facts and returns an accurate picture of them. If the facts are poorly understood, the resulting judgment will be poor. If the response is either insufficient or excessive, the judgment will also be, for that reason, poor. Therefore, strength comes from sound judgment and sound judgment is achieved by strength.

Finally, *strength*, it is said, is necessary to support what *wisdom* contrives. This alludes again to *left/right* symbolism. Wisdom is abstract and needs structure and form to be practical. Understanding formalizes thought and makes it expressible. In kabbalistic symbols, *Gevurah* is directly below *Binah*, so *strength* derives directly from *understanding*. It's true our beliefs are strengthened by understanding. It's also true the other way. Going back to a point made earlier, it's difficult to grasp something that is not, or cannot be, clearly defined. Strongly defined concepts, those that mark clear parameters, are much easier to understand. So *strength* is a quality of the *understanding* required to turn imagination, impulse, or feelings into formal thoughts and ideas which can be made real as speech and action.

Beauty

The third column, the one that symbolically "balances" the other two, is called *Beauty*. Contemporary usage of the word beauty makes this symbol, in some ways, the least obvious of the three. Everybody can easily understand the symbols of *Wisdom* and *Strength* to represent the obvious virtue of being *wise* and *strong*. But *beauty*? Is it a virtue to be *beautiful*? In the Western hemisphere, where both Freemasonry and Kabbalah emerged, the concept of *beauty* has been discussed and developed since the earliest Greek philosophers. Anciently, *beauty* was understood to imply a properness of fit. To Pythagoras, an early Greek philosopher and mathematician, *beauty* was the awareness of a type of natural balance, perceived in sound as harmony, or by sight as symmetry and order. The physical display of balance and order was made a symbol of a general rightness, an accordance with the laws of nature and divine will. Beauty might describe not just someone's appearance, but their personality, character, talent, or intellect.

Wisdom and strength, symbolically *right* and *left*, are sometimes compared to *water* and *fire*, and at others, to the right and left hands. Though different, in both cases, it's beauty which "balances" them. Strength or power, like fire, if it's uncontrolled, is a source of destruction. As water keeps fire from becoming destructive, wisdom keeps strength from becoming a tool of injustice. Conversely, as the fire stirs and warms the water, without strength, wisdom will never take form or exert any positive influence. Though opposed to each other, Wisdom and Strength are not enemies. Imagine wearing mittens and trying to pick up a snowball with one hand. Without the other mitten to stop it, the snowball keeps rolling away. However, using two hands, the snowball is easily captured. The second hand allows the force exerted by the first to be focused and applied to the snowball. It turned the potential into actual practical strength. This is also like Adam and Eve.

Beyond the dubious "rib" translation already mentioned, the Bible story of Adam and Eve suffers from several other poor renderings in English. Genesis twice tells that God wanted to find "*a help meet*" for man. This archaic expression, as it appears in the King James Bible (1611), is, in more modern translations, usually rendered as a "*helper suitable*" for him. The Hebrew expression is *ezer kenegdo*. The word *ezer* (עֵזֶר) means help. The second word, *kenegdo* (כנגדו), means *opposite* or *set across from*. God did not seek an agreeable servant for man, but a helpful opposer. The traditional "*help meet*" story of the Bible, like the "*rib*" story, obscures the symbolism of cooperative and complimentary "*sides*," not just of humanity, but of everything that exists or occurs. In the next example, the verse is explained not to refer to actual men and women at all, but to the *sephirot,* and the interdependence of complimentary parts that sustains the whole world. This is represented by the pillars of *Wisdom*, *Strength*, and *Beauty*.

Zohar I, 48b, Parashat Be-Reshit

> *YHVH Elohim fashioned* הצלע *(ha-tsela), the side, that He had taken from the human into a woman, and He brought her to the human* (Genesis 2:22).

> Rabbi Shim'on said, "It is written: *Elohim understands her way, He knows her site* (Job 28:23). This verse bears numerous nuances, but *Elohim* הבין *(hevin), understands, her way* corresponds to what is said: ויבן יהוה אלהים *(Va-yiven YHVH Elohim), YHVH Elohim fashioned, the side*—namely, Oral Torah, who contains a way, as is said: *who makes a way through the sea* (Isaiah 43:16). So, *Elohim understands her way.*

> *He knows her site.* Who is *her site?* Written Torah, containing knowledge.

Rabbi Shim'on is explaining the verse (*Genesis 2:22*) where God makes a woman from the rib of a man. The word *tsela* is, instead of *rib*, given the more accurate translation of *side*. The word *adam* is equally improved, rendered as *human*, rather than *man*. Shim'on invokes two other verses to start his explanation.

First, he connects the phrase *"fashioned the side"* with another verse, *"Elohim understands her way"* (*Job 28:23*). The word ויבן *va-yiven* is here translated *fashioned* but often rendered as *built* or *made*. He relates *it* to the similar word, הבין *hevin, understands.* Doing so, he equates *"fashioned the side"* with *"understands her way."* The *side*, Shim'on adds, is *Oral Torah*, a kabbalistic reference to *Malkhut*, which, he says, contains a *way*. The verse from Job continues, *". . . He knows her site"* (*Job 28:23*).[52] Shim'on teaches that *her site* refers to the *Written Torah*, an allusion to *Tif'eret*.

What however did Shim'on mean that Oral Torah contains a way? To explain, he cites another verse; *"who makes a way through the sea"* (*Isaiah 43:16*). The *sea*, as we know, is *Malkhut*, just identified as "Oral Torah." Shim'on suggests the "way through the sea" indicates the *sephirah Yesod*, which connects *Tif'eret* and the others to *Malkhut*, the sea.

In Kabbalah, every word is susceptible to symbolic interpretation. Fittingly, the rabbi proceeds through the verse in its entirety, explaining each word and phrase.

Zohar I, 48b, Parashat Be-Reshit (cont.)

YHVH Elohim—a complete name, arraying Her with all, so it is called both Wisdom and Understanding, for it bore the complete name entirely—*YHVH Elohim*—consummating two names.

The *complete name, YHVH Elohim*, the LORD God, was explained earlier. The two names used together symbolize the union of right and left, specifically *Hokhmah* and *Binah, Wisdom* and *Understanding*. This is given to show that the *Shekinah* derives from both sides and lacks nothing of the divine substance.

Zohar I, 48b, Parashat Be-Reshit (cont.)

הצלע (*Ha-tsela*), *The side*—speculum that does not shine, as is said: ובצלעי (*Uv-tsal'i*), *At my stumbling, they rejoiced*...(Psalms 35:15).

A play on the word *tsela* invokes a kabbalistic tradition concerning the humility of *Malkhut*. The *speculum that doesn't shine*, is a reference to the *Shekinah* emanating no light of its own, and only reflecting that of the other *sephirot*. The Hebrew root צל (*tsl*), also means *to stumble*. Rabbi Shim'on alludes to the incomplete nature of *Malkhut*, associating *the side* (*ha tsela*) with stumbling; *at my stumbling, they rejoiced* (Psalms 35:13).

Zohar I, 48b, Parashat Be-Reshit (cont.)

That He had taken from האדם (*ha-adam*), *the human*—for She issued from Written Torah.

Another of the many nicknames for *Tif'eret* is *ha-adam, the man*. By this alias, *Tif'eret* represents the primordial model for humanity. The symbol of *Malkhut, the side* which had been fashioned, being taken from the human (*ha adam*), refers to *Malkhut* issuing from *Tif'eret*. This symbolism, whereby *Malkhut*, the *Oral Torah*, issues from Tif'eret, the *Written Torah*, illustrates a key concept. The *Oral Torah* issues from the *Written Torah*, not like a child issues from a parent, but rather how a result issues from an intention or a reality issues from an idea. *Oral Torah* is the living, interactive *Law*, applied and adjudicated here on Earth, in the mouths and hearts of the people. The *Written Torah* is the fixed and unwavering Truth, the essential *Law*, written in the *Heavens* and reflected in the *Earth*.

Zohar I, 48b, Parashat Be-Reshit (cont.)

Into a woman—to be joined to the flame of the left side, for Torah was given from the side of Power. לאשה (*Le-ishshah*), *Into a woman*—to be אש ה (*esh he*), fire of *he*, bound together as one.

The verse continues, . . . *fashioned the side that He had taken from the human into a woman.* Shim'on explains that *into a woman*, refers again to the joining of *right* and *left* and says this is because the Torah, "was given from the side of Power." The Hebrew word לאשה (*le ishshah*), *into a woman*, he reads instead as לאש ה (*le esh he*) *to the fire of he.* Already explained, the pillar of *fire is the left column*, commonly named after *Gevurah (Strength, Power)*. The rabbi, with this reading, invokes, as a symbol, the Hebrew letter ה (*he*). This letter appears twice in the ineffable name, יהוה (*YHVH*). The first *he* refers to *Binah, Understanding. Binah* is the supernal feminine, the *Mother* of all. She, at the top of the left column, is the true source of both *Strength* and *Judgment.*

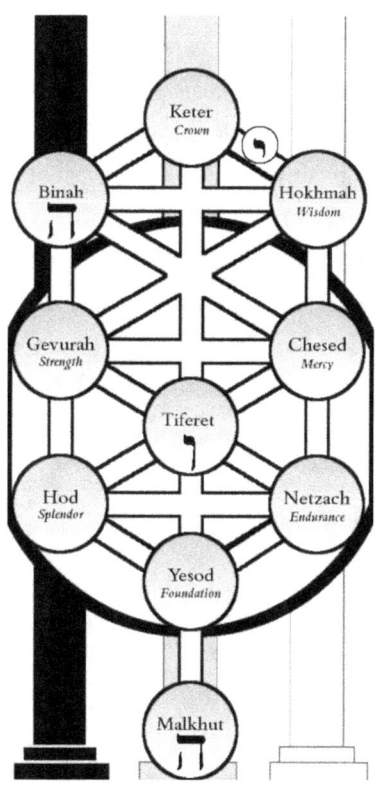

Binah, *understanding*, is the immediate source of the left pillar, including Gevurah, *strength*, also known as Din, *judgment*. Binah, "the divine feminine," is the ideal for Malkhut, "the divine female," therefore both are represented by the letter *he*.

However, Shim'on seems to refer instead to the second occurrence of the letter *he*, the last letter of the divine name. This symbolizes *Malkhut*, the *Shekinah*, the divine female, the *Daughter* or the *Bride*. The *lower he*, reflects the *upper he*, *Binah*, and so the *Shekinah* receives its defining qualities from the *left*. So the *fire of he* describes *Malkhut's* emergence from the pillar of fire, the left column of *Gevurah*, the side of *Power*.

Zohar I, 48b, Parashat Be-Reshit (cont.)

And He brought her to האדם (*ha-adam*), *the human*—for She should not be alone but rather embraced by, joined with Written Torah. Once She joins with Him, He will nourish and adorn Her, providing Her what She needs.

Finally the verse concludes, *and He brought her to the human*. Not the first *boy-meets-girl story*, kabbalists understand this to symbolize the union of *Malkhut* with *Tif'eret*. Like every story in the Bible, even the "rib" story is another account of the *sephirot* and the triumph of existence over non-existence. Shim'on again uses the symbol of *Torah*, describing the *Oral Torah* being united with and "*embraced by*" the *Written Torah*. Once they are united, "*He will nourish and adorn Her, providing Her what She needs.*" This is another repetition of the familiar *above/below* or *Heaven/Earth* theme. However, a thorough consideration reveals its practical value and perhaps something worthy of greater reflection.

Angels go up and down Jacob's Ladder at Bath Abbey. Robert Vertue, an English architect and master mason, worked on the construction beginning in 1499.

Jacob's Ladder

The Pillar of Beauty, the reconciliation of Wisdom and Strength, deserves further thought. In Kabbalah, both *Tif'eret* and *Malkhut* reside on the middle column of the *Tree of Life*. This pillar extends both higher and lower than either the right or left ones. From this illustration, it's suggested that *Beauty* is both the *cause* and the *effect* of the balance between *Strength* and *Wisdom*. That is, *Wisdom* combined with *Strength* results in *Beauty*, and equally, *Wisdom* and *Strength* come from *Beauty*.

As an *idea*, *Beauty* considers appropriateness and correctness of fit. Like the invisible inspiration that moves an artist, it's the standard of rightness that determines where to place the equilibrium between opposites. This ideal of *Beauty* appears to the mind. It inspires, compels, and ultimately causes the balance. Beauty, in an *applied* sense, is the thing of beauty, presented not to the imagination, but to the senses. This is the idea made real. It's the order and symmetry of parts, assembled and working in perfect complement to each other. This physical *beauty*—manifestation of the ideal—is the *result* of the balance. Beauty, though often named last, is, in this way, also the first.

Earlier, the virtues of faith, hope, and charity were discussed. Charity was explained as a charitable feeling toward others, the masonic virtue of Brotherly Love. I symbolized charity as the foundation upon which hope and faith were supported. Now, it should be considered that charity is also an act, or an offering. It takes physical form in the real world. People perform charity and make contributions to charity. Charitable behavior is the result of charitable thoughts and feelings. Charity is, like Beauty, both the cause and the effect. It's not, however, one word for two things. Charity is one thing with two sides and those sides cannot be separated. The heavenly idea of *Charity*, the charity of the mind and the heart, is made real on Earth by acts of *charity*, the charity of the hands and feet.

In Kabbalah, the connection between Heaven and Earth is often symbolized by the biblical account of *Jacob's Ladder*. As the story goes,

Jacob is traveling between cities. Stopping and resting after sunset, he dreams of a ladder, extending from Earth to Heaven, traversed up and down by angels. From the top of the ladder, he hears a voice reaffirming to him the covenant made by God with his grandfather, Abraham. In amazement, Jacob proclaims the spot to be "the house of God" and "gate of heaven." This is the well-known bible story. By now, some of Kabbalah's symbols should be recognizable. The ladder reaching from *Earth* to *Heaven* refers to the connection between *Malkhut* and *Tif'eret*. Heaven and Earth aren't merely tied to each other, they have a relationship. They interact and respond to each other in dynamic ways.

The following example expands the relationship between the *world above* and the *world below*. In the *Zohar*, Creation is an ongoing process. More than just reflecting or resembling each other, the worlds above and below are involved in the mutual benefit and support of one another.

Zohar I, 57b-58a, Parashat Be-Reshit

> *My spirit shall not abide in humanity forever* (Genesis 6:3).
> Rabbi El'azar said, "Come and see: When the blessed Holy One
> created the world, He fashioned this world to perform as above.
> When the inhabitants of the world are virtuous, walking in the
> straight path, the blessed Holy One arouses the spirit of life above
> until that life reaches the site where Jacob abides. From there life
> flows until the spirit is drawn to this world in which King David
> abides. From there blessings flow to all those below. Since that
> supernal spirit is drawn and conducted below, they are able to
> endure in the world. So, לעלם (le-olam), *forever*, without a ו (vav)—
> עולם (olam), *world*, of King David, spelled without a ו (vav). For
> when that spirit flows into this world, from there blessings and life
> issue to all, to be sustained. Now that humans sinned, all was
> withdrawn to prevent the spirit of life from reaching this world,
> benefiting, sustaining those below.

Rabbi El'azar introduces a concept central to Kabbalah. A divine flow, by which life is sustained, circulates between above and below. Human virtue, he explains, stimulates the "spirit of life" which moves toward and eventually is drawn into the world below. Humanity is not a helpless bystander, but an active partner in the maintenance of the world. The life-giving spirit is conducted from Heaven to Earth by way of the *sephirot* and the paths connecting them. In return, the virtuous thoughts and actions of the people are carried upward through the same network, increasing the divine sustenance.

El'azar says, when the people are virtuous, divinity is stirred until "life reaches the site *where Jacob abides.*" His explanation relies on the kabbalistic practice of identifying specific persons from the Bible with the *sephirot*. Many important characters refer not simply to historical or legendary persons, but to specific *sephirot*. *Jacob* refers to *Tif'eret.** King David, also mentioned, is a symbol of *Malkhut*. David, the prototype King of Israel, naturally symbolizes *Malkhut*, usually translated as *kingdom*. So, from *the site where Jacob abides*, *Tif'eret*, the spirit is drawn to *this world* where *King David* abides, *Malkhut*.

The rabbi finishes with a clever kabbalistic device. As no defect can be ascribed to the Bible, anything that looks like an error is interpreted to have special meaning. Variant spellings, with missing or added letters, and other grammatical problems, are symbolic themselves. El'azar addresses one such *misspelling* in the verse he's explaining.[53] Reading, *my spirit shall not abide in humanity for ever* (*Genesis 6:3*), his focus is on the Hebrew word עולם (*olam*) which can mean either *eternity* or *world*. Here, לעלם (*le-olam*), literally *to eternity*, is rendered as it usually is; *for eternity*, or, more simply, *forever*. The rabbi noting a textual detail however, suggests a different understanding. He reads instead, "my spirit shall not abide in humanity *in the world.*"

In this verse, the word עלם (*olam*) is spelled deficiently, missing the letter *vav* (ו). This letter symbolizes *Tif'eret*. The fact that it is missing from the word *olam*, *the world*, symbolizes the *Shekinah* separated from *Tif'eret*. He explains this is a consequence of human misdeeds and wrongdoing. Virtuous acts of the people increase the outpouring of heaven, but when the people are not virtuous, blessings are withdrawn.

---

* *Tif'eret*, among its many nicknames, is also called *Truth*. Its association with Jacob comes from a kabbalistic reading of the verse, "*you will give truth to Jacob*" (Micah 7:20).

Every action we take impacts the world around us. The simple idea at the heart of Freemasonry, that virtue fuels the harmony of society while vice disrupts it, seems intuitive. This belief empowers humans to make a difference. Every person is an active player, directly involved in the operation and upkeep of the world. Of course this is symbolic, but the lesson, once again, is practical. Virtue and honest effort generally lead to success, while cheating and taking short-cuts tends to miss the mark in the end.

In Kabbalah, the union of *Tif'eret* and *Malkhut*, the symbolic marriage of *Heaven* to *Earth*, is a principal theme. If it seems overly dramatic to place all of existence in the balance of this celestial union, remember Kabbalah and Freemasonry are symbolic. One underlying message is Masonry, like anything, exists first as an ideal. If the reality of it becomes disconnected or too removed from the ideas that define it, then something else will have replaced it, and Masonry will not exist. To bring reality continually closer to the ideal of perfection is the mission of freemasons. *In the beginning, God created the Heavens and the Earth*. To join *Heaven* and *Earth* is to bring the whole world into being. To separate them is to turn out the lights on everything.

The Righteous One is the Foundation of the World

A reading of Proverbs 10:25, gives us another kabbalistic tenet. Traditionally, the verse is read as "*The righteous one is an everlasting foundation.*" Again, the word *olam* (עוֹלָם), means both *eternity* and *world* or *universe*. Translated here as *everlasting*, the verse is instead read by kabbalists as "*the righteous one is the foundation of the world.*"

Zohar I, 245b, Parashat Va-Yhi

Happy are the righteous in this world and in the world that is coming, for upon them stand those above and below! Therefore, *The righteous one is foundation of the world* (Proverbs 10:25)— written unspecifically. Mystery of all: *Righteous one* is *foundation of the world* above and *foundation* below, and Assembly of Israel is encompassed by *righteous one* above and below.

Daniel Matt, translator of the *Zohar*, provides this explanation in his footnote on this verse:

> "*The righteous one . . .*—written unspecifically . . . Scripture leaves the identity of *the righteous one* intentionally vague, so that the term can apply both to *Yesod* (known as Righteous One) and to a righteous human. Above, *Yesod* (Foundation) is an extension of *Tif'eret* and thus consummates the union with *Shekinah*; below the righteous human performs the vital function of stimulating *Shekinah*. Thus, *Shekinah* is embraced above and below by *the righteous one.*" (Matt, *Zohar*, vol. III, p. 503, n. 902)

As with nearly all things kabbalistic, this idea is said to be true "*above and below.*" In the *world above*, it refers to the sephirah *Yesod, foundation,* which is known as '*the Righteous One.*' *Yesod* directly connects *Malkhut* to *Tif'eret* and the rest of the *sephirot*, and is the middle rung of *Jacob's Ladder*. In the *world below*, it's the righteous among the people, those few who sustain the blessings of heaven for the sake of everybody. The *Shekinah,* called *Assembly of Israel,* is therefore said to be "encompassed by the *righteous one* above and below." That is, by *Yesod* above and the people below.

Divine Providence

The *Shekinah*, identified with *Malkhut*, is the concept of a *divine presence* in the world. The name comes from a Hebrew word for *tent* or *dwelling* and is traditionally understood as God literally dwelling among the people. More rationally it refers to the aspect of divinity accessible to humans. This vital element of Kabbalah, is also an important symbol in Freemasonry. The details attached to anyone's particular concept of a *divine presence*, are, in the end, only important to them. For some, a divine presence actively intercedes in the everyday lives of themselves and others. Some see the presence of divinity clearly portrayed in the infinite variety of beautiful and wondrous sights, sounds, and feelings we experience. The perfection of mathematics or the precision of the laws of the universe, are, to some, the picture of divinity present in the world. All of these perspectives are not just valid, they are valuable.

As uncomfortable as it is to imagine, as counterintuitive as it seems, and as contrary to our experience, some scientists propose that free will is an illusion. Astrophysicist Brian Greene is one such person who believes that the laws of the universe make the idea of free will impossible.[54] Everything that ever has happened, is happening, or will happen was already "decided" at the moment of the Big Bang. From that point, all of the energy and every particle that exists was set on its way, its course inalterable, predetermined by natural law. As Greene points out, that includes every particle and all of the energy involved in your brain functioning and therefore every thought you've ever had or will have, including those you're having now.

Of course, this interesting position by Greene, a brilliant scientist and writer, is a fascinating thought experiment, but not very practical. It seems very unlikely that the network of relationships that make up humanity—families, friends, communities, countries—could survive without the idea that each person is acting according to their own free will. Even the most brutish imagining of humanity can't abide a world where people aren't responsible for their own behavior. All groups—from immediate families to complex societies—depend on each member receiving credit and being accountable for their actions. Whatever it is that we experience and call free will, even if it is as Professor Greene says, not exactly free, we have no other way to understand it. The enormous span of events from the beginning of time to your most recent thought, is far beyond contemplation. It feels like free will and, more importantly, we have to treat it—both our own and others—like it is free will.

The world we live in and experience, provides only a glimpse of a greater, incomprehensible, reality. That fact seems unavoidable. Relative time and space, quantum uncertainty, eleven-dimensional reality—these concepts of modern science only reinforce the unfathomable mystery of the universe. The distance between the truth that avails itself to the mind, and the truth that lives in the heart, is often difficult, and at times impossible, to traverse except by faith. Sometimes we trust our *minds* and we call it *reason*. Other times we trust our *hearts* and call it *intuition*. In both cases we are relying on faith. Neither of the functions of the human brain, the one we call *reason* or the one called *intuition* is, in reality, what it's experienced to be.[55] Reason seems to be a logical process. It very often is not. Intuition is even more mysterious, inexplicable even by the one experiencing it. That doesn't mean that we stop relying on our reason or our intuition. The fact that we don't fully understand how or why our experience is formed, doesn't fundamentally change the experience. Just as importantly, the fact that we experience something, even regularly, doesn't change the fact that we may not actually understand it.

This world of uncertainty is the stage for human experience. Trying to close the gap between the Truth we seek above and the truth we can't avoid below. Spanning the ladder between worlds.

Zohar III, 159a - 159b, Shelah Lekha

Come and see: The blessed Holy One has three worlds, in which He is hidden. First world—that supernal one, most concealed of all, which is neither known nor glimpsed, except by Him.

Second world—a world that is linked with the one above. This is the one by which the blessed Holy One is known, as is written: *Open for me the gates of righteousness; this is the gate to YHVH* (Psalms 118:19–20). This is the second world.

Third world—the world below them, where separation exists. This is the world in which supernal angels dwell, and the blessed Holy One exists there and does not. He is there now, yet when they wish to see and know Him, He departs from them and is not seen . . .

Similarly, *In the image of God He made the human* (Genesis 9:6), so he has three worlds. First world—this world, called World of Separation, and the human being exists there and does not. When they wish to see him, he departs from them and is not seen.

Second world—a world that is linked with the higher world. This is the terrestrial Garden of Eden, which is linked with another, higher world . . .

Third world—a supernal concealed world, hidden and secret, unknown by anyone, as is written: *No eye has seen, O God, but You, what You will do for one who awaits You* (Isaiah 64:3).

This passage describes the divine presence in the world, explaining three dimensions of God's existence. The first is transcendent. An unknowable realm beyond human contemplation. The world *before* time and space, completely unimaginable in real terms. The second is the world of the *sephirot*, where the attributes of divinity are revealed and can be understood or perceived. This, says Rabbi Yehuda, is the world "by which the blessed Holy One is *known*." The third is the world where separation exists, the material world; a world separated from divinity and full of separate things. Here it is said God "exists and does not" and "He is there now, yet when they wish to see and know Him, He departs from them and is not seen . . ." This turns out to be a pretty good description of divine presence in the real world. For those who can conceive it, the Divine is everywhere present in the beauty and splendor of nature. However, for those who want to see it with their eyes, it is not.

Yehuda then describes three worlds of human interaction with divinity. These noticeably have an inverse correspondence to the divine worlds. The first of these is the third world of the Divine—the world of separation. Poetically described in nearly identical terms, human existence is quite different from transcendent being. The same words used to describe divine incorporeality—"[He] exists there and does not"—in this case, refer to human mortality. Human life is fleeting. A person exists one minute and then does not.

The second human world is said to be the way by which the higher world is known. Yehuda calls this world the *Garden of Eden*, a symbol elaborated elsewhere in the *Zohar*, involving a series of *halls* or *palaces* through which departed souls are imagined to pass.[56] None of the *Zohar* is meant to be understood literally. This story is no exception. Though the plain language suggests an afterlife experience of the soul, like everything else, it's a symbol to interpret. The reference being to "the *souls* of the *righteous*" when they have "*departed* from *the world*" could easily be a metaphor for the soul-searching or transcendental journey of deep or inspired contemplation. For some this could be prayer, for others, meditation.

The second world is the middle rung of the ladder connecting *Heaven* and *Earth*. In the second world of the Divine, the Truth is revealed. In that same world, from the human perspective, it is received and understood. Here, the mysteries of the Divine become *knowable* through the laws of the Universe. Unlike the lowest world, this is not a world of sight and sensation, it's a world of *knowledge* and *understanding*.

In the material world below, the *Law* is experienced. Its effects are felt. In that ever-changing world of time and matter, the divine Truth, though present, is difficult to recognize. In the second world its fuller implications are understood. Knowing the *Law* is knowing a part of that Truth which is divine. Therefore, Yehuda teaches from the second world "the other," higher world is known.

The highest palace, the third world of human experience, is the world beyond earthly contemplation. Here lie all the secrets of the universe, unimaginable except to divine wisdom. In this world, by divine providence and our own virtuous effort, the highest mysteries are made, if not attainable, at least, approachable. As we saw with earlier examples of infinite size, the unknown, and even the unknowable, can be contemplated according to those attributes which can be known about it.

The divine presence, understood this way, is a constant part of human experience. Wherever humans exist, divinity can be found. In the world of sensation, the divine laws are in action, and we see beauty and strength, discern good from bad, and prefer what is true and just. This is the foundation of both self-improvement and a charitable view of others. In the world of thought, the Law is understood, and applied generally to our thinking. We can imagine what is possible, making room for hope.

Above both is a world into which neither passion nor knowledge can purchase entry. This is the world of faith. Here abides, not certainty, but trust; the belief that what ought to happen will finally happen. The ultimate Truth cannot, in the end, be denied. This is the mysterious source of the inspiration called *will*. It's this inspiration, known only to man and divinity, the very light by which good is recognized, providing the seed of charity.

From these and countless other incarnations of divine presence, comes the idea of *Providence*. Providence includes everything experienced as part of life, the good along with the bad. The same facts that led Dr. Greene to doubt the freedom of free will, allow for a rational concept of providence. After all, everything that ever happened to you or will ever happen to you, everything you've ever had, wanted, or lost, and everything you've ever thought or *will think*, was *provided* at the instant of the Big Bang.*

For humans, life is lived and experienced as a balance of free will and providence. Life is *both* what you make of it *and* the hand you're dealt. Positive and negative, the experiences that define your life, consist, in part, of what happens to you, and in larger part, of *how you respond* to what happens to you.

---

* Only if you believe in science.

A feature common to all masonic lodges are the pillars, styled after those placed at the entrance to Solomon's Temple, which each lodge is said to symbolize. *Clockwise from top-left*: artist rendering of Solomon's Temple, a lodge in Cornwall, England, a lodge in Western Australia, a lodge in Astoria, New York

The Tabernacle and the Temple

Freemasonry modeled its lodges, however approximately, after the legendary King Solomon's Temple. The account of that building's construction comes from the Book of Kings. The temple was believed to have been built on Mt. Moriah in Jerusalem, some time before the end of the sixth century BCE. Its ruins have never been discovered, but the spot where it's said to have stood, the Temple Mount, remains a holy site. Whatever the historical or archaeological facts happen to be, the concern to Freemasonry is academic. Masonry sees King Solomon's Temple, and each masonic lodge, as a symbol of the universe.

The story of Solomon goes like this: upon becoming king, he's invited by God to his choice of gifts. Solomon chooses, not power or riches, but wisdom. This pleases God who grants it to him—along with wealth and honor—to a degree "*as no king who was before you ever had and none after you will have.*" Solomon asked for wisdom and received so much of it that his name became synonymous with it. In Kabbalah, the universe was created with wisdom. In Masonry, the temple that symbolizes the universe was built by Solomon, a symbol of wisdom.

The Tabernacle

To simply say a masonic lodge is a symbol of the universe, doesn't tell the whole story. The Temple of Solomon, was built as a *dwelling* for God. This makes each lodge a symbol, not just of the universe, but of the divine presence abiding in the universe. In the following passage from the *Zohar*, the verse presented could seem to refer to the Temple. However, the reference is actually to the first dwelling place arranged for the divine presence, the Tabernacle constructed by Moses in the wilderness, which is said to be the model for King Solomon's Temple.

Zohar II, 59b - 60a, Raya Mehemna[57]

> It is an obligation to build a sanctuary below on the pattern of the
> Temple above, as it is said *"The place, O Lord, which You have
> made for Yourself to dwell in"* (Exodus 15:17), for it is necessary to
> build a sanctuary below and to pray within it every day in order to
> serve the Blessed Holy One, because prayer is called "service." And
> as for the temple, one must build it in the most beautiful fashion,
> and adorn it with every kind of adornment, for the assembly below
> matches the assembly above.[58] The Temple below is patterned on
> the Temple above, one matching the other. All the adornments of
> the Temple, its rituals, its vessels, and those who minister there, all
> match the one above.

Compared to previous examples, the symbolism of this passage is easy
to interpret. It directly addresses the symbolic work which freemasons
call *building the Temple.* Though the verse specifically refers to the
Tabernacle of Moses, the symbolism is no different. In the story of the
Tabernacle, Moses had just led the escape from Egypt, but the people
were now wandering the desert with no permanent home. The Tabernacle
was a tent that could be transported and assembled as they moved from
place to place. Symbolically, it might represent the place we provide for
divinity when our lives are in flux. When life goes relatively well, it is
much easier to be thankful and thoughtful, but when life is tumultuous,
the same grace and perspective can be difficult to maintain. However,
it's during those tough times—when we tend to be more concerned
only about ourselves—that we might benefit most from keeping a view
broad enough to include others.

Moses and the children of Israel legendarily roamed the wilderness
for forty years. During this time, the divine presence, the *Shekinah,*
dwelled with them in the Tabernacle. The Temple, kabbalists say, could
not be built until stability was brought to the kingdom. There is symbolic
significance to this. The *Tabernacle* is the model upon which the *Temple*
will later be patterned. Consider then, the way you behave or respond
during difficult and trying circumstances, will be the model for what
you do when your life is going well. Making excuses for being unkind,

undisciplined, unsympathetic, or ungrateful because the going is tough makes it difficult to resume correct behavior when the time comes.

The Tabernacle was a tent and could be moved from place to place. This was very practical when wandering in the wilderness. King Solomon's Temple, on the other hand, was a palace. Practically speaking, in any new journey expect to *wander in the desert* for a while, and carry around a tent. Don't start building a palace the first place you come to rest. As you're learning, be nimble, open-minded, and responsive to new information. Keep in mind how much you have to learn. Avoid forming convictions too quickly or before knowing all the facts. Your Temple symbolizes the moral and ethical structure where you'll safeguard and develop your faith and keep your relationships and reputation in order. Be sure, and only erect your Temple on sacred, and solid, ground.

The Temple of Solomon

The Temple, like the Tabernacle, is a symbol of divine presence. Masonic lodges are, likewise, such a symbol. However, Masonry also sees the Temple as a symbol of another sort. The construction of the Temple is a metaphor for life. This book has already discussed different symbolic representations of life, including journeys through time, from morning to evening, and space, from east to west. Building symbolism, however, is substantively different.

In a symbolic journey, whether through time or space, one location is departed, and another one is arrived at. The end state is a complete or thorough transformation from the original condition. *Building* symbolism is not the same. A building doesn't start as a foundation and transform into a roof. Each piece, each story, is a layer on top of the previous ones, and a building is only as stable as its supporting structure. Symbolically, it speaks not to change but to another type of progress; growth and development. Building on top of what came before. Becoming, not different, but more complete.

The symbol of *building the Temple*, speaks to the personal development central to the ideals of Freemasonry and the hope for a just and charitable world. The building and the builders are united symbolically. Each builder must be trusted to do his best work and must rely on the others to do the same. Only this way can every tier of the building be trusted, to squarely sustain what will be built on top of it, and to be true to the foundation and floors that support it.

The *Zohar*, it should no longer be surprising, has its own interpretation, presenting the *building of the Temple* as another symbolic account of the *sephirot*. This next passage, one of the last to be presented, seems to, in an appropriately kabbalistic way, summarize all of the others. Touching on many of the symbolic terms already introduced from the *Zohar*, Rabbi Shim'on explains the miraculous construction of the Temple, which kabbalists say *built itself*, providing instruction to the builders as they worked.

Zohar I, 74a, Parashat Noah

Rabbi Shim'on said: . . . "*The House when it was being built . . .* " (1 Kings 6:7)—When it arose in the will of the Blessed Holy One to fashion glory for Its glory, the desire arose from thought to expand—expanding from the site of concealed thought, unknown, expanding and settling in the throat, a site continuously gushing in the mystery of the spirit of life. When thought expanded and settled in this site, that thought was called אלהים חיים (*Elohim Hayyim*), Living God: *He is Living God* (Jeremiah 10:10).

It sought to expand and reveal Itself further; thence issued fire, air, and water, merging as one. Jacob emerged, Consummate Man, a single voice issuing audibly. Hence, thought, having been concealed in silence, was heard revealing itself.
Thought expanded further revealing itself, and this voice struck against lips. Then speech issued, consummating all, revealing all. It is perceived that all is concealed thought, having been within, and all is one.

Once this expansion ripened, generating speech through the potency of that voice, then *The House, when it was being built.* The verse does not read *when it was built*, but rather *when it was being built*, at every single interval.

Stone perfected, as it has been explained, for it is written "the crown with which his [i.e. Solomon's] mother has crowned him" (Song of Songs 3:11).

Quarry, Journey—issuing from within, dwelling, journeying outside; issuing from above, dwelling, journeying below.
No hammer, ax, or any iron tool was heard—other, lower rungs, all dependent upon it, neither heard nor admitted within when She ascends to unite above to be nourished there. This is [the meaning of] *"when it was being built."*

The expression examined here—the house when it was being built—comes from the account of the construction of Solomon's Temple in the first book of Kings. In this example, the Hebrew word בהבנתו (b'hibanotu), is at the source of the verse's famously odd wording. The word, literally translated, is something close to, *in its building of itself.* From this, the King James version and others give, *In the house when it was in building.* Most modern translations provide *when it was being built*, which is the form Rabbi Shim'on chooses for this kabbalistic explanation. He begins in a familiar way, recalling the creation of the world from the moment it "arose in the will" of the Great Architect. As he descends through the *sephirot*, starting with the unknowable *Keter*, the mysterious *Will*, Shim'on makes use of practically all the symbolic themes and ideas presented in this book.

Hokhmah, Wisdom, is again the beginning, the divine first thought. Creation proceeds to *Binah, Understanding,* who is here called the throat, the origin of speech, alluding to the worlds of creation advancing from a realm of *thought* to a world of *language,* and to God *speaking* light into the world. Shim'on refers to the symbolism of the divine names, invoking the name *Elohim Hayyim, the Living God.*[59] He revisits the trio of fire, water, and spirit (*Gevurah, Chesed,* and *Tif'eret*), from which the heavens were made. Jacob is mentioned, another symbol of *Tif'eret.* Here, he is called the *Consummate Man,* the perfect model of humanity, the image *above* from which human beings were created *below.* Returning to the symbol of speech, the voice which started in the *throat* is now knocking against the *lips*, to be made into sound and to take shape in the world. The original unexpressed will is created in thought, then formed into language, before being made into speech. Everything is connected, all is one. The unusual wording of the verse, Rabbi Shim'on explains, refers to this multi-step process. It doesn't read *when it was built*, but rather, *when it was being built*, in various stages.

Shim'on then offers another interpretation of the phrase. Going through the verse part by part, he explains each one individually. The entire verse reads:

> *The House, when it was being built, was built with stone finished at the quarry, so that no hammer or chisel or any iron tool was heard in the temple while it was being built* (1 Kings 6:7).

He starts with the phrase *stones finished at the quarry*. The Hebrew word מסע (*massa*), means both *quarry* and *journey*. Shim'on prefers the latter for his explanation. These are stones made ready *by the journey*. The next phrase, *no hammer, ax, or any iron tool was heard*, is explained. The "tools of iron" are elements of the material world, which receive blessings when *Shekinah* is dwelling below. However, when She ascends to be reunited with *Tif'eret*, these *"tools of iron"* cannot join her. So, it's explained, such sounds were not heard *in the House when it was being built*. That is, they were not heard by *Malkhut*, while She was being replenished with the blessings of *Tif'eret* above.

Both explanations provide symbols worth considering. The Rabbi's first presentation reminds us that the work of *building the Temple* is ongoing. It's not completed in one step, it's progressive. The Temple isn't *built*, it's *building*, and the process continues through life. His second explanation is philosophical and spiritual, but also very practical. Life is taxing. Dealing with the realities of the world often requires some withdrawal from it.

Many derive physical, spiritual, and psychological benefits from meditation, prayer, or other forms of separating their thoughts from the world around them. Such perspective taking is regularly described in ascendant or transcendent terms. Reaching a *higher level* or *leaving the world behind*. In intellectual pursuits, there is often a benefit to taking a *higher perspective*; seeing more of the *forest*, less of the *trees*. Thinking in *broader terms*, seeing the *big picture*, getting the *fifty-thousand foot view*; all symbolically express the same thing. A situation, act, or idea can't be fully appreciated until it is understood in a full context. Plenty has been done that seemed at the time to be either good or bad, but was later realized to be the opposite.

It's easy to let our judgment be clouded by personal interests and concerns. This is the practical lesson. It's often tempting to do, not what's best, but what's best for ourself as an individual. Masons should make it their practice to resist this temptation and instead, always try to do what is right and fair. Placing some distance between yourself and the situation provides a better perspective from which to do that. By disallowing the noise from those "tools of iron," you eliminate any prejudice, passions, or interests that might detract from your honest consideration of truth, charity, relief, and justice.

Closing

Freemasonry has, as an institution, survived for centuries. However, its place in the world can never be guaranteed. The group, at one time remarkably popular, may now be on the verge of disappearing. This is the position in which Masonry, with its symbols and stylized language taken directly from the King James Bible, finds itself today. What was long considered the miraculous and true history of humanity, is now widely looked upon as a mythological tale. Previous generations who regarded the Bible as authentic history, had little reason to discover symbolic meaning in the verses, any more than students today look for symbolic meaning in the Great Depression or the Taft administration. However, as organized religion has, in recent generations, diminished in Western culture, Freemasonry lost relevance in a society that now only understands its symbols as outdated and odd.

How good and how pleasant

As I said in the beginning of this book, Masonry is important. Its teachings and traditions have, throughout history, encouraged and provided a safe space for the open and honest discussion of the truth, in science, philosophy, and religion. The symbols by which Masonry has, for centuries, taught its lessons and maintained its identity, are being allowed to decay. If Masonry is going to play a part in the future, relevant meaning must be restored to these symbols. As Kabbalah showed by adapting the Bible to reflect a contemporary understanding of the world, symbols can be reinterpreted and reexplained. In the case of Masonry's symbols, if there is any hope of them again being meaningful, they must be.

I conclude with the following passage from the *Zohar*. The message is relatively clear, so I don't provide any further explanation. The point of this book is, after all, not for me to provide my interpretations of symbols, but to show that symbols are meant to be interpreted and how that might be done. In the end, my understanding of these symbols may only to be truly valuable to me. It's up to you to interpret them for yourself as meaningful signs of the *Wisdom* that contrives, the *Strength* that supports, and the *Beauty* that adorns the true *Temple*, the one being built within each faithful heart, and which reflects the glory and harmony of the whole universe.

Zohar 3:7b

> He opened again, saying, "Look, how good and how pleasant is the dwelling of brothers together!"...Out of love for them, the blessed Holy One called them servants...Afterward He called them children...Afterward He called them brothers...and because He called them brothers, He wanted to place His abode among them and not withdraw from them; then it is written: Look, how good and how pleasant is the dwelling of brothers together!

So mote it be.

Notes

1. Alexander Towey, "*The Rise, Decline, and Renaissance of Freemasonry in the United States during the 20th and 21st Century*" (California State University San Marcos, 2022), https://wp.csusm.edu/freemasonryusa/wp-content/uploads/sites/4/2022/11/ToweyAlexander_Fall2022.pdf., p. 18

2. Towey, p. 20

3. Towey, p. 20-21

4. Towey, p. 24

5. W.L. Wilmshurst, *The Masonic Initiation*, 1924, p.12

6. Wilmshurst, p.12

7. John Bizzack Ph. D., *Island Freemasonry: The Final Bastion of the Observant Lodge*, 1st ed. (2017)

8. Christopher Hodapp, "*How the 1960s Really Killed American Freemasonry's Future,*" July 3, 2019, https://www.linkedin.com/pulse/how-1960s-really-killed-american-freemasonrys-future-hodapp/.

9. Towey, p.31

10. If current membership trends continue, some projections show the current model for Freemasonry failing by the year 2040, less than 20 years from the time of this writing. John Hinck, *Understanding the Decline in Participation in Fraternal Organizations: A Mixed Methods Approach*, 2018, p.4

11. *Harper's Magazine*, 11/30/1944, How men behave in crisis

12. Elaine Howard Ecklund and Jerry Z. Park, "*Conflict between Religion and Science among Academic Scientists?,*" Journal for the Scientific Study of Religion 48, no. 2 (June 1, 2009)

13. Charles Sanders Peirce, *Peirce on Signs: Writings on Semiotic* (UNC Press Books, 1991).

14. Hugo Mercier and Dan Sperber, *The Enigma of Reason* (Harvard University Press, 2017).

15. Rex Richard Hutchens and Albert Pike, *Pillars of Wisdom: The Writings of Albert Pike*, 1995.

16. "Mary Hicks witch of Huntingdon." (2018, April 11). *Early Modern Medicine*. https://earlymodernmedicine.com/mary-hicks-witch-of-huntingdon/

17. Stephen Hawking, *Brief Answers to the Big Questions* (Bantam, 2018).

18. *Tao Te Ching*

19. Genesis 1:3

20. Genesis 1:1-2

21. Newton's Law of Motion

22. For an example, refer to Dr. Shannon Grimes's 2018 work *Becoming Gold* where the earliest historically valid alchemist, Zosimos of Panopolis, extols the value of cooperating with and not resisting the laws of the universe, which in his very Egyptian way he understood to regulate the conduct of gods as well as humans.

23. Benedict de Spinoza, *Ethics*, trans. Edwin Curley (Penguin, 1996).

24. Newton couldn't explain how two objects with mass exerted this force, as if by "magic" on each other across distance. His belief that space was inert did not allow him to imagine, as Einstein did, that the objects are not interacting with each other directly but that both are interacting with the fabric of spacetime.

25. The Strong Force binds together the protons and neutrons of an atom's nucleus. The Weak Force accounts for atomic decay.

26. Freemasons should consider the symbolic Working Tools of the first degree.

27. The sun was long considered, along with the moon, to be one of the seven planets.

28. Different alchemists would provide slightly varying lists, but according to Agrippa, the seven correspondences are as follows: Sun = gold, Moon = silver, Saturn = lead, Jupiter = tin, Mars = iron, Venus = copper, Mercury = quicksilver

29. *Guide for the Perplexed*, 2:26

30. Psalm 111:10 "Fear of the Lord is the beginning of wisdom"

31. The Jerusalem Targum, the Aramaic translation of the Hebrew bible, begins "In wisdom…"

32. Joel Hecker, *Zohar*, ed. Daniel Matt, Pritzker Edition, vol. 11 (Stanford, California: Stanford University Press, 2016, 665 n. 102).

33. J. Hecker translates "etched etchings." Here I preferred Tishby/Goldstein's plainer translation "drew sketches" to illustrate the point of God as a designer.

34. Hecker translates "etched and traced." I preferred Tishby/Goldstein's "sketched and formed" for consistency. See note 33.

35. Hecker translates "inscribed impressions." I preferred "sketching designs" again for consistency. See note 33.

36. Hecker translates "etching." I preferred "sketching." See notes 33 & 34.

37. This is according to a tradition in Kabbalah where the letter vav, by its numerical value of six, was equated both to *Tif'eret*, the sixth sephirah, and also collectively to the six lower sephirot—*Chesed, Gevurah, Tif'eret, Netzach, Hod,* and *Yesod.* See page 144.

38. There are, in reality, several methods of calculating the value of a word according to Gematria. Adding the values of each letter is the simplest.

39. For the sephirot as the names of God, see page 159; also Gikatilla, *Gates of Light*

40. Tishby cites Babylonian Talmud, Hullin 127a: "Everything existing on land exists in the sea, except the weasel."

41. Daniel Matt explains "if a biblical law is stated in general terms, followed by particular instances and then followed by another generality, one may derive only things similar to those specified. For example, Deuteronomy 14:26 states: You may spend the money on anything that your appetite desires (generality), cattle, sheep, wine, or intoxicant (particularity), or anything that your appetite seeks (generality). According to the principle of kelal ufrat ukhal, one may purchase things other than those specified, but only if they are food or drink similar to those specified." *Zohar,* v.I, p.122

42. There are other arrangements by which the sephirot are visualized which are seldom referenced. Concentric circles are one well-known example.

43. A central symbolic feature of Judaism is male circumcision. The site of this mark of the covenant is represented by the sephirah Yesod, foundation.

44. Earth, air, fire, and water are primary symbols in alchemy. Despite a legacy of alchemical expertise attributed to Jewish practitioners, there is little trace of authentic alchemical influence in the *Zohar* or elsewhere in kabbalistic literature.

45. Babylonian Talmud, Hullin 60b, Matt, *Zohar,* vol. VII, p.229, n.71

46. *Sifrei Devarim* 26:10

47. YHVH is not normally pronounced but is generally replaced with the word *Adonai,* Lord. Some Christian traditions attempt to render it literally as *Jehovah* or *Yahweh,* resulting in translations that give *Jehovah of Armies,* etc.

48. Some Christian sects, notably the Jehovah's Witnesses, do not observe the Jewish tradition regarding the ineffability of God's name.

49. Ecclesiastes 1:6, "Moving toward the south, circling toward the north, round and round goes the wind and on its rounds the wind returns."

50. So did the early Church Fathers, who adopted them as Christian virtues.

51. The Greek *phrónēsis* corresponds to the Hebrew *binah* in several places

in the Septuagint translations.

52. The full verse of Job 28:23 reads "God understands its ways. He knows its place." However, the Hebrew word היא (hu), may be translated as he, she, or it, so Rabbi Shim'on reads it "Elohim understands her way, He knows her site." referring to the Shekinah.

53. The idea of a misspelling implies a correct spelling. Spelling, even in early modern language, was not yet standardized. This is especially true of ancient languages. This variant spelling in this example is called deficient because it's spelled without the Hebrew letter *vav*.

54. Brian Greene, *Until the End of Time: Mind, Matter, and Our Search for Meaning in an Evolving Universe* (Vintage, 2020).

55. Mercier & Sperber, *Enigma of Reason*, 2017

56. *Zohar* I, 39a, Heikhalot Bereshit

57. This passage is from a Zoharic work called the *Raya Mehemna*, or *Faithful Shepherd*. It is considered to be a late addition and, as such, is excluded from some editions of the *Zohar*. The Pritzker Edition, from which comes most of the translations in this book, does not include the *Raya Mehemna*. The translation included here is taken from Isaiah Tishby's *Wisdom of the Zohar*.

58. I preferred the more general term *assembly* (my translation) over the word *synagogue* as the English translation of the Hebrew phrase *bet knesset*, literally "house of assembly."

59. This expression, *Elohim Hayyim*, usually refers to the sephirah *Yesod*. Here, however, it's used in connection with *Binah* which has a mystical connection with *Yesod*. For more on the relationship between *Binah* and *Yesod* see Gikatilla, *Gates of Light*.

References and Bibliography

Agrippa, H. C. (2021). *Three books of occult philosophy*. Simon and Schuster.

Bianchi, U., & Stefon, M. (1999, July 26). Dualism. *Encyclopedia Britannica*. https://www.britannica.com/topic/dualism-religion/Themes-of-religious-dualism

Bizzack, J., Ph. D. (2017). *Island Freemasonry: The Final Bastion of the Observant Lodge* (1st ed.). Macoy Publishing. (2017)

Chandler, D. (2022). *Semiotics: The basics*. Routledge.

Contributors to Wikimedia projects. (2024a, January 26). *Maimonides*. Wikipedia. https://en.wikipedia.org/wiki/Maimonides

Contributors to Wikimedia projects. (2024b, January 29). *Age of enlightenment*. Wikipedia. https://en.wikipedia.org/wiki/Age_of_Enlightenment

DeepL Translate: The world's most accurate translator. (n.d.). DeepL.Com. Retrieved February 26, 2024, from https://www.deepl.com/en/translator#el/en/

Eckhart. (2005). *Meister Eckhart, from whom god hid nothing: Sermons, writings, and sayings*. Shambhala Publications.

Ecklund, E. H., & Park, J. Z. (2009). Conflict between religion and science among academic scientists? *Journal for the Scientific Study of Religion, 48*(2), 276–292. https://doi.org/10.1111/j.1468-5906.2009.01447.x

Edge, E. (n.d.). *Metal melting temperatures of common engineering materials*. Retrieved August 7, 2024, from https://www.engineersedge.com/materials/metal_melting_temperatures_13214.htm

Einstein, A. (1961). *Relativity: The Special and the General Theory*. Three Rivers Press.

Green, A. (2004). *A guide to the zohar*. Stanford University Press.

Greene, B. (2003). *The elegant universe: Superstrings, hidden dimensions, and the quest for the ultimate theory*. W. W. Norton & Company.

Greene, B. (2020). *Until the end of time: Mind, matter, and our search for meaning in an evolving universe*. Vintage.

Hammer, A. (2020). *Observing the Craft: The pursuit of excellence in masonic labour and observance* (5th ed.). Mindhive. (2010)

Hawking, S. (2018). *Brief answers to the big questions*. Bantam.

Haymond, B. (n.d.). *Nüwa and fuxi in Chinese mythology: Compass & square – temple study*. Retrieved July 9, 2024, from https://www.templestudy.com/2008/09/17/nuwa-and-fuxi-in-chinese-mythology-compass-square/

Hecker, J. (2016). *The Zohar* (D. Matt, Ed.; Pritzker Edition, Vol. 11). Stanford University Press.

Hodapp, C. (2019, July 3). *How the 1960s really killed American freemasonry's future*. https://www.linkedin.com/pulse/how-1960s-really-killed-american-freemasonrys-future-hodapp/

Home of freemasonry. (n.d.). United Grand Lodge of England. Retrieved January 29, 2024, from https://www.ugle.org.uk/

Hutchens, R. R., & Pike, A. (1995). *Pillars of Wisdom: The writings of Albert Pike*.

Huxley, A. (2012). *The perennial philosophy: An interpretation of the great mystics, east and west*. Harper Collins.

Lachower, Y. F., & Tishby, I. (1991). *The Wisdom of the Zohar: An anthology of texts*.

MA, R. B. (2022). *The foundations of modern freemasonry: The grand architects: Political change and the scientific enlightenment, 1714-1740*. Liverpool University Press.

Maimonides, M. (2012). *The Guide for the Perplexed*. Courier Corporation.

Mary Hicks witch of Huntingdon. (2018, April 11). Early Modern Medicine. https://earlymodernmedicine.com/mary-hicks-witch-of-huntingdon/

Matt, D. (2003-2016). *The Zohar* (Pritzker Edition, Vols. 1-9). Stanford University Press.

Mercier, H., & Sperber, D. (2017). *The Enigma of Reason*. Harvard University Press.

Midrashic literature. (n.d.). Encyclopedia.Com. Retrieved February 7, 2024, from https://www.encyclopedia.com/religion/encyclopedias-almanacs-transcripts-and-maps/midrashic-literature

Morris, R. (2003). *The Last Sorcerers: The Path from Alchemy to the Periodic Table*. Joseph Henry Press.

Neill, W. N. (1923). The Last Execution for Witchcraft in Scotland, 1722. *The Scottish Historical Review*, 20(79), 218–221. https://doi.org/http://www.jstor.org/stable/25519547

Patai, R. (1994). *The jewish alchemists: A history and source book*. Princeton University Press.

Peirce, C. S. (1991). *Peirce on signs: Writings on semiotic*. UNC Press Books.

Platts-Mills, B. (2024, July 2). The forgotten priest who predicted black holes – in 1783. BBC. https://www.bbc.com/future/article/20240626-the-priest-who-predicted-black-holes-in-1783

PS review of freemasonry. (n.d.). PS Review of Freemasonry. Retrieved January 30, 2024, from http://www.freemasons-freemasonry.com/regius.html

Rovelli, C. (2022). *Helgoland: Making sense of the quantum revolution*. Penguin.

Sifrei devarim 26:10. (n.d.). Retrieved September 17, 2024, from https://www.sefaria.org/Sifrei_Devarim.26.10?lang=bi

Sivan, R., & Levenston, Dr. E. A. (2009). *The New Bantam-Megiddo Hebrew & English Dictionary, Revised.* Bantam.

The 1723 constitutions. (2020, September 15). 1723 Constitutions. https://www.1723constitutions.com/

The Hanoverians. (n.d.). The Royal Family. Retrieved January 29, 2024, from https://www.royal.uk/hanoverians

Thermodynamics. (1999, July 26). *Encyclopedia Britannica.* https://www.britannica.com/science/thermodynamics/The-second-law-of-thermodynamics

Towey, A. (2022). *The Rise, Decline, and Renaissance of Freemasonry in the United States during the 20th and 21st Century* [California State University San Marcos]. https://wp.csusm.edu/freemasonryusa/wp-content/uploads/sites/4/2022/11/ToweyAlexander_Fall2022.pdf

Webmaster. (n.d.). *The Zohar: Pritzker Edition.* Retrieved February 4, 2024, from https://www.sup.org/zohar/

Wilmshurst, W. L. (2007). *The Masonic Initiation, Revised Edition.*

Wolski, N. (2016). *The Zohar* (D. Matt, Ed.; Pritzker Edition, Vol. 10). Stanford University Press.

Image Credits

The following images have been reproduced in this book with proper attribution and in accordance with their respective licenses. Where applicable, public domain justifications are provided based on U.S. copyright law and Wikimedia Commons/Flickr Commons guidelines.

Public Domain Images (Wikimedia Commons):

Shriners – Harris & Ewing; Library of Congress, via Wikimedia Commons. Public domain. https://commons.wikimedia.org/wiki/File:Shriners_LCCN2016892419.jpg

Portrait of Pope Clement XII – Unknown artist, via Wikimedia Commons. Public domain. https://commons.wikimedia.org/wiki/File:Retrato_del_papa_Clemente_XII_(Universidad_de_Salamanca).jpg

G7 Summit Family Photo (2024) – European Union, via Wikimedia Commons. Public domain. https://commons.wikimedia.org/wiki/File:EU_@G7_Summit_2024-Family_photo(06).jpg

Gottfried Wilhelm von Leibniz – Unknown artist, via Wikimedia Commons. Public domain. https://commons.wikimedia.org/wiki/File:Gottfried_Wilhelm_von_Leibniz_(2).jpg

Meister Gerard – Unknown artist, via Wikimedia Commons. Public domain. https://commons.wikimedia.org/wiki/File:Meister_Gerard.jpg

Moses Maimonides – Wellcome Collection, via Wikimedia Commons. Public domain. https://commons.wikimedia.org/wiki/File:Moses_Maimonides._Photogravure._Wellcome_V0003789.jpg

West Window of the Chapel, New College, Oxford – Georg Siegmund Facius, via Wikimedia Commons. Public domain. https://commons.wikimedia.org/wiki/File:Georg_Siegmund_Facius_-_West_Window_of_the_Chapel,_New_College_Oxford,The_Virtues-Justice-B1977.14.10351-_Yale_Center_for_British_Art.jpg

Woman Teaching Geometry – Unknown artist, via Wikimedia Commons. Public domain. https://commons.wikimedia.org/wiki/File:Woman_teaching_geometry.jpg

Anderson's Constitutions – Freemasonry historical document, via Wikimedia Commons. Public domain. https://commons.wikimedia.org/wiki/File:Anderson%27sConstitutions.jpg

Marriage of the Sun and Moon (Rosarium Philosophorum) – Historical alchemical illustration, via Wikimedia Commons. Public domain. https://commons.wikimedia.org/wiki/File:Marriage_Sun_Moon_-_Rosarium_Philosophorum_Griemiller.jpg

God the Geometer – Unknown medieval artist, via Wikimedia Commons. Public domain. https://commons.wikimedia.org/wiki/File:God_the_Geometer,_Codex_Vindobonensis_2554,circa_1220-1230(29304249070).jpg

Creative Commons Licensed Images:

Recycling Symbol – Public domain SVG, via Wikimedia Commons. Licensed under CC0 1.0 Universal (CC0 1.0 Public Domain Dedication). https://commons.wikimedia.org/wiki/File:Recycling_symbol2.svg

Lorenz Attractor – Mathematical visualization, via Wikimedia Commons. Licensed under CC BY-SA 3.0. https://commons.wikimedia.org/wiki/File:Lorenz_attractor_yb.svg

Adam Kadmon - Created by Derol Frye, adapted from an original image by Jakob Suckale, licensed under CC BY-SA 3.0. Source: Wikimedia Commons.

Flaticon Icons (Used Under Free License with Attribution)

Diskette Icon – Icon made by Yogi Aprelliyanto from www.flaticon.com. https://www.flaticon.com/free-icon/diskette_1451766

Phone Call Icon – Icon made by Those Icons from www.flaticon.com. https://www.flaticon.com/free-icon/phone-call_733464

Voicemail Icon – Icon made by Google from www.flaticon.com. https://www.flaticon.com/free-icon/voicemail_61156

Video Film Icon – Icon made by fjstudio from www.flaticon.com. https://www.flaticon.com/free-icon/video-film_92346

Author-Created Images:

Screenshot of an article from the Edinburgh Caledonian Mercury (April 4, 1743). Original newspaper content is in the public domain. Digital scan accessed via newspapers.com.

Etz Chaim, Tiferet Six – Created by Peter Cardilla. All rights reserved.

Three Pillars, Tetragrammaton Sephirot, and Binah Malkhut – Created by Peter Cardilla, adapted from an original image by Paolo D'Angelo, licensed under CC BY-SA 4.0. Source: Wikimedia Commons.

Photograph of painting Psalm 107 by David Friedman – Photograph taken by Peter Cardilla of artwork in his personal collection. Used with permission from the owner.

Additional Notes

Some images have been cropped, resized, or adjusted for clarity and formatting. Any modifications do not affect the original licensing terms. Images licensed under Creative Commons Share-Alike (CC BY-SA) retain the same license and can be shared with proper attribution.

Peter Cardilla is a father, husband, computer scientist and freemason. On top of twenty-five years as a software engineer, he has spent the past two decades studying, thinking about, and lecturing on Kabbalah. Active in several masonic bodies and recipient of numerous degrees, Peter is a Past Master of Confidence Lodge #110, in Soquel, California and a member of Paideia Lodge #852, a Traditional Observance lodge in Santa Cruz, California. A decorated member of the Societas Philologi (S.R.I.C.F.)–a masonic philosophical society–and a 2022 Grand Commander's Fellow for the Scottish Rite of Freemasonry, Peter brings his own unique perspective to the symbols of Freemasonry and symbolism in general.

The on-again/off-again songwriter and his wife live in Santa Cruz where they raised their son and now contend with an adorable shih tzu and an unwieldy schedule.

The Beginning is Wisdom, his first book, combines his insights on science, philosophy, Freemasonry, and secret traditions–particularly Kabbalah–with his ideas for how these fit together in today's world.